Dale Kruse practiced dentistry for 25 years in Northwest Colorado. After retiring he took up building homes as a hobby and to keep his mind and body healthy. This allows him to spend time with his two sons in a family business. These professions allowed him to explore the mountains and rivers in expedition style. He currently lives in a remote valley near the Flat Top Wilderness, surrounded by the nature he passionately explores to this day.

PRIMORDIAL SOUP

AN EXPLORATION INTO RISK TAKING

DALE KRUSE

AUSTIN MACAULEY PUBLISHERS™

LONDON • CAMBRIDGE • NEW YORK • SHARJAH

Copyright © Dale Kruse (2021)

Ordering Information
Quantity sales: Special discounts are available on quantity purchases by corporations, associations, and others. For details, contact the publisher at the address below.

Publisher's Cataloging-in-Publication data
Kruse, Dale
Primordial Soup

ISBN 9781647507688 (Paperback)
ISBN 9781647507671 (Hardback)
ISBN 9781647507701 (ePub e-book)
ISBN 9781647509460 (Audiobook)

Library of Congress Control Number: 2021916661

www.austinmacauley.com/us

First Published (2021)
Austin Macauley Publishers LLC
40 Wall Street, 33rd Floor, Suite 3302
New York, NY 10005
USA

mail-usa@austinmacauley.com
+1 (646) 5125767

To Scott Fisher, a good friend lost on Everest and to Dave Mondeau, who I spent so many adventures with and to my wonderful wife, Terry Doherty, who shared with me wholeheartedly in my explorations. Also, Angela, who motivated me to write this book.

My wife, Terry, who helped with my story recollection and rereading.

I'm exploring the mindset that brings a person to take on risks. Does the adventure define who we are or, do we define the adventure? Inadvertent things happen when we go places and thus the adventure. The degree of our choices, however, can also define the adventure. What brought me to these moments? When asked why climb Everest, Hillary remarked, "Because it's there".

Is it that simple? No, it's not. I think it's a primordial instinct that lies in all of us to take risks. Otherwise, we would never have evolved. I call it my primordial soup. My genetic road map from evolutionary times.

James Ramesy Ullman wrote, *"There is no growth in what is safe and comfortable."* When we get that 'feeling of relief' from an adventure, we feel that growth. Accomplishment stimulates a powerful primordial drug within us. It then leaves us yearning for more; addiction.

My friend, Scott Fisher, died on the 1996 Everest climb, and I have always carried with me the responsibility of possibly contributing to his downfall with altitude as I will explain soon enough.

I exclaim here today that maybe one should lose this primordial soup over time especially with such a past of close calls. A learning curve would seem to take over with time. However, as you will see below, the primordial soup is a thick one.

My Metanoia

The harshest month of the year is truly January. I have never floated the river in January. Why not take a river trip if you want to experience the cold weather and conditions of snow? I have been down the river in snowstorms many times, and it is beautiful. The snow spindrifts off the smooth entrada slopes and falls over the Wingate cliffs below. A whole new look to the canyon walls is at your gazing pleasure all day long. So, why not go?

I knew it would have to be a solo trip. Who else would want to go and sit in the cold? Crazy.

I knew there may be ice dams, but I had been watching the river with nothing big forming yet, just ice on the banks. I knew I could walk out on the railroad tracks that followed the canyon to Westwater. I knew Black Rocks would present the highest risk due to the slow water and back eddies. So, I took the risk. Twenty-five miles of unknown at every bend. My worst fears in the restless sleep the night before came true.

A sunny first day with highs in the thirties and lows in the mid-teens. Ice slush chunks floated past me, so I rowed and kept up. It was my plan to row all day just for the exercise. Also, it is usually a three-day trip and I planned to do it in just two. I must add that the snow on the cliffs was breathtaking and the geese and ducks were in the hundreds as I witnessed a maelstrom of wings and noise when they took off in flight. The ice along the bank started to grow and twenty to thirty feet of ice sheets in the back eddies became more common. But still a good flow down the middle. I made it all the way to black rocks, 17 miles by 3 p.m. That's when my pulse and attention skyrocketed.

Black Rock is an incredible piece of geology. The river cuts down through many layers of history of sandstone, and then at this spot, it hits the bottom of time, the bedrock of mother earth, the schist. Hard black, smooth, house size rocks that the river has sculpted through are an impressive sight, an ominous site even on a summer day. It's an 'Oh my God' moment when you realize you are viewing the canyon from top to bottom, 500 million years of time. The formation of planet earth. The current is slow here, and it twists and turns in eddies and whirlpools.

I floated in the current and passed the upper section of the dark monoliths, scanning constantly the banks and the growing ice along them. I knew every oar stroke I made at this point I must have a ditch out plan in a stroke or two. No room for second chances. The current would not allow you to move against it. I shake at the keyboard even now as I write about this next moment.

A large rock sits in the middle of the river, and the river disappears around it. There are cliffs on river left and too much ice on the bank river right.

There is a snow cap that seems to extend across the river to the large rock. I misguidedly think for a moment that the river has to go around it and through it even though I can't see it.
I float on for another moment, losing my quick ditch options by the second. I'm going for it. I'm up against the cliff on the left now, trying to peer around the rock, looking for a slot through the ice. Instantaneously, I shock myself into reality that I can't make it.

I pull back hard against the current and bang my oars into

the cliff. I must get separation from the cliff and further out into the current to row back in the flow. I know I'm not allowed one missed stroke at this point; if so, the current will be unforgiving and I'll be trapped.

I pulled hard with anger at myself. How did I allow this to happen? Rowing upstream is not easy, but I was making progress. Pulling over into the jumbled rocks on shore is still a task when solo. You must jump quickly and hold the boat and not break a leg or slip into the freezing water as well. All a big risk. Not to mention your boat floating down without you in it. I tied up. I was in a hurry to see what lay below, and my heart was racing. I yelled as strong as I could a cuss word or two in order to communicate with myself the predicament I was in. I also realized I was on the wrong side of the river in case I had to walk out. Too many cliffs below and above.

I might have to swim the river to get to the other side.

The scout downstream was horrifying. A huge chunk of ice two feet thick extends across to the black rock damming the river. A massive back eddy pushes against the ice, and current rushes against the rock. The ice slush from upstream slams into the blockage and swirls violently in circles. Some ice disappears below the ice shelf, maybe finds its way out some two hundred feet downstream. I stood in awe and pictured myself in this swirling mass and torrent. Trapped. There would be no escape. But I am living still.

Darkness was coming soon, and I knew I must not delay my own rescue. So I tackled the next problem. I must get to the other side of the river. The railroad tracks were my only way out.

Pulling over to the other side was not possible in this spot. The current would push me, and I would land on the other bank where ice was ten feet out from shore. I had to row upstream again around another rock to a new eddy, the only way out.

My first attempt left me back in the same spot as I banged my oars too much on the rock I needed to get around. I had to get further out into the current and row harder. I was tired but adrenaline was my friend and a fear of failure was motive enough. Finally, I was upstream another thirty feet. No way to go up anymore, so I must cross the current and make a landing before I am swept down steam into whatever. Don't want to think about it.

I made it. And I am still alive.

I felt out of danger at this point, and now it was all a logistical problem, except for keeping warm. Cold hands, core temp felt cool, shivers, and feet were a concern. I had not eaten all day in order to make time, and my nerves were shot. Focus on the problem. I had to get the tent set up and get in my bag or run around.

I grabbed my bags and climbed up the embankment one hundred feet, sliding back one foot for every two taken. Felt warmer. I needed to see if I could portage the raft or if I should walk out the eight miles. I pressed on. Hiking down the railroad tracks, I saw just how massive the ice jamb was and another below that one. After a half mile, I found a spot where I could lower equipment down the embankment and reach the river. It was here I would set up a rope and lower stuff back down.

I made the decision to try portage, and knew I had nowhere else I had to be and plenty of food and a good sleeping bag. I had the spot device which allows text anywhere in the world so I informed my wife, Terry, of my plight and plan etc. I was also warmer now with the hike and decided to start immediately without eating. No time to waste. Going to get dark. The oar frame was the big 'if'.

I spent the next several hours unpacking the coolers into the dry bag and packing loads half a mile down the river then back up river for another load; three or four loads. Slept hard that night, despite camping a mere ten feet from the tracks, the only flat spot. I counted four trains that night as the tent shivered with their passing.

The sun was up at seven and so was I. Heavy on my mind was the weight of the oar frame, and I was anxious to see if I could haul it the full distance. Among the myriad of boulders, the site was strewn with coolers and boxes and oars and tubes. But, finally, the oar frame stood bare, for even the sideboards I had cut off. The straps were too frozen to get through the buckles.

I moved it six feet at a time, standing in the middle, lifting and walking over the boulders. Resting, then through some stubborn tamarisk, resting and to the base of the slope. Resting. It was too hard to carry gear up this slope, so I rigged a rope to pull stuff up about forty feet. To get myself up the slope, it was by hands and knees crawl. Ice was at the top of the slope, so I cut out a foothold and pulled hard four feet, resting, panting. Four feet, resting. Finally done, I put the frame on the tracks sideways, rigged up a harness, pulled like a bull in a rice field thirty steps, rested, panted. This went on for a half mile and took a big bite out of the day. Down at the other end, I just let it slide down on its own. Then I carried it six feet at a time to the river some 100 ft. away. Done.

I had to force myself to eat as there was no appetite whatsoever. Even though the exertion would have demanded more nutrients, I did not feel hungry. There was no sun. The river was in a shroud of low foggy clouds. It was cold. I was warm with the fruit of my labor. It took me a total of nine hours in two days to haul one-mile round trip the two coolers, metal dry box, three oars, three dry bags, two tubes, and four loads of bags from the coolers, boxes, and the floorboards. Plus, the damn oar frame! Mental notes to myself dictated that I bring less stuff next time. The trains went by, and I waved to the passengers and wondered what they thought. Apparently, they reported me to the sheriff.

Almost done with my portage, a big truck on railroad wheels came up on me quickly. Unlike the approach of trains, I did not hear it coming. Out pops a sheriff who is of course interested in my well-being, but he is on a mission to find the reported sighting of hanging deer. Even though the sheriff and company are going the right direction for my portage, they refused to even carry a few boards for me down the tracks and drop them off for me. I'm exhausted, really tired but just say, "Good luck". Later, I think to myself and analyze the new world order. These are younger men by 25 years or more. I am nearly 68 and the task lay all around me. But they saw only what?

Another day of idiotic recreational behavior that happens all the time these days.

Let him suffer. He will learn. Problem is I have been in so many quagmires. Learning must be slow for me.

On their way back an hour or so later, they stop and ask me many questions about deer and guns and a hanging hide and really check me out. The game and fish warden is there, too. "Yes, I have a gun."

"Is it on you now?" asks the warden.

"No, it's a .22 pistol, down at the raft." etc., etc.

Finally, they decide it's an erroneous report about me and my site and tell me not to camp so close to the tracks. I look around for another site and see no one anywhere and say, "Okay."

I tell them, "Before you call me an idiot, wait until you are in your truck, on your way back."

We laugh. It's cold. They are cold in the light wind and mist with no hats on. They would be shivering in a few minutes. They are on their way fast, heated truck and all.

You think the story ends here, but I must tell you that there is a new penetrating coldness which the mist has created. The river is shrouded in a wet dampness creating an ethereal atmosphere. I am re-rigged, and it's getting late the second day, 2 p.m.

I oar in the mist constantly to keep warm. The low clouds make it tough to see far down the canyon, especially for a one-eyed man. I could bring out the down suit I brought, but I need every minute to get to the take out before dark. It's simply my goal.

My hands get too cold to oar and I must stop to shove them in my armpits. I am underdressed and my core feels cold. The sun must have set because it's eerie out now. I have trouble seeing the gravel bars which scare me. If I land on one, I would have to wade cold water with a borderline body temperature as it is. I am still around.

The take out is the last scary encounter I have. The boat ramp lies behind a pushy current and an ice shelf about three ft. out from shore. The water drops off fast here. It's cold. It's dark. I am cold and starting to shiver. My fault. I can stop and dress up, but I don't. I know I'm okay. No one is around and it's quiet. Very still, and I feel the solitude and remoteness of my situation.

I pull hard and place the tubes up on the ice shelf, but by the time I am ready to jump ashore, the boat has shot out from the ice into the current rendering me incapable of making a six-foot jump without a total bath of cold water. It's freezing out. I'm starting to shiver more. Need my sleeping bag. Need to get on shore.

After several failed attempts to get landed and rowing backup stream each time, I finally pull up to it sideways, throw the rope on shore, make a quick full out leap over the ice and hit shore. Meanwhile, the boat is quickly on its way downstream with the help from my push-off, like a bullet from a gun. With my sleeping bag in it!

The rope was a bit wet when I grabbed it. Coils of rope disappearing fast into the dark water like a snake rushing to find a watery escape. I did not slip on the ice; I did find my balance; I did make the few steps I needed to catch the rope.

I am still around, and around and around.

I set camp and waited for Terry in the morning. Yet, one more surprise, I must not forget.

The morning is brisk and twinkly with frost in the air. A dozen large black objects silhouette the branches in the tree above. As the light finally grows from the darkness, I discover the large turkeys roosting and realize it's my Metanoia. I will surely come back someday, as one of them.

Next year, I will do it differently! Want to go?

I

Scott lost his energy and succumbed to the harshest of elements on the mountain. I could not have imagined this scenario as Scott and I climbed the rolling and winding path toward Everest base camp. We camped for a day at a small village and took off for a quick hike up a hillside, scaling a rocky peak with grand views of the Himalayan mountains.

Twenty-two thousand feet, Ama Dablam soared above us and we reflected and pondered about our climb there several years before. Reminiscing of days gone by with joyous laughter from two healthy young climbers, creating an everlasting bond.

Dale, left, and Scott.

I had spent so many days with Scott on the trail in expeditions, in different countries, in a tent, on a cliff, or hanging from ice falls that he had become one of my best friends. How at this moment, at this magnificent spot, with all this laughter could one think that it would be my last emotional connection with him? This turned out to be the last real singular time we spent together. In two weeks, he would be gone.

Scott was renowned for his ascents of the world's highest mountains and made them without supplemental oxygen, including K-2 and Everest and Lhotse. He had climbed six of the highest peaks on as many continents. He had helped raise hundreds of thousands of dollars for charity in his climbs. Also cleaned up tons of trash from the littered Everest slopes.

Early in his career, he broke an ice ax while climbing Bridal Falls in Telluride and tumbled down the vertical cliff hundreds of feet. Although he stabbed himself with the pick, he was primarily unhurt. He was unstoppable. He also had fallen into a crevasse on K-2 and tore his rotator cuff but made the summit with one good arm two weeks later. He also had to save two other climbers who required help as a result of altitude sickness. Something that he would eventually do for me in the weeks ahead.

*

The first time I wondered about or fantasized about Everest might have been in 1973. Reports of big huge expeditions going up the highest mountains was impressive news back then. The first American on Everest was Jim Whittaker in 1963, ten years after Hillary's first ascent. By contrast, the first American woman was on our expedition in 1996. Many peaks had remained unclimbed even until a year before our expedition. For example, Scott Fisher was the first American to climb one of the highest peaks in the Himalayas, Lhotse.

You have to place yourself back then. You can't look at

climbing Everest from the perspective of current news and the commonality of things today. Today, I'm not sure it is even ethical to climb Everest. In the last five years, 32 sherpas have died out of a few hundred available, making it the most high-risk job in the world. Climbers risk the lives of others to help them achieve their goals. The world is a much smaller place today. Money speaks louder than experience.

Back then, things were being discovered for the first time. Unclimbed mountains were everywhere; the first descents of rivers had not occurred. The first spaceship, *Voyager 1*, was sent to the outer planets. People still believed there could be Martians living on Mars. Einstein's theory had been just completely proven by radio waves. It was still a time for exploration.

In 1970, I remember thinking to myself how could people live and camp at altitude in snow and cold for so long? So, I had to try. I bought an old army bag and a good down coat. I hitched a ride up to Lake Eldora ski area and punched holes in the snow some 50 ft. off the road and up a rocky point.

There in the wind and falling snow, I slept out at altitude, my first experiment to see if I would feel the attraction to the elements. It was enabling.
I hitch hiked back in time for classes in Boulder.

Tales of expensive big expeditions to climb remote places were making news. It seemed insurmountable to think a person could gain enough experience to do such a thing back then. Or even get in the right circles to be invited on such a trip. Only the best were allowed to go.

This, of course, has changed big time. I would have to say that in 1996, the year I went to Everest, that it changed more than ever, forever. Back then, you were on a team for an expedition, not a guided trip somewhere. But, at least, I prepared for years to get the experience I thought I needed. Not so today.

After my classes that day, I went and bought a pair of snowmobile boots and a cheap A-frame tent. I was excited and planned my next winter camping trip. This time I would hike further into the woods and set up camp. I found a friend that suffered with me in the wet cold and then frozen night. This happened many weekends for many years to come. I did immediately progress to x-country skies and thus became a backcountry traveler.

I felt it necessary to become an erudite on mountaineering. I read a lot on the subject. The story of Peter Schoening on K-2 was quite remarkable.

Pete was tied with five climbers that were now in rescue mode. They had a fellow in a sleeping bag with pulmonary edema at 25,000 feet in a storm. While trying to traverse an ice slope lowering the sick climber, one climber fell down the slope into three other climbers on the team. They then fell onto a rope holding the injured climber held by Pete. Quick thinking and speed saved the climbers. He shoved his ice axe into the ice and slammed his boot on top of it. The rope held all the climbers while hanging there during the self-rescue that followed the injured climber cut his rope in order to help save the rest of the climbers.

Pete gave up the trip with Hillary to be the first on Everest. He chose the K-2 climb instead. This all happened in 1953. Forty-three years later, at my age now, 68, he attempted Everest. We were on the same Everest team. He was also the first to climb Gasherbrum-1, one of the 14 world's highest peaks. Also, the first to climb Mt. Vinson in Antarctica in 1966. I was with a climbing legend walking the slopes of the highest mountain in 1996.

While in dental school, I came to know some others that wanted to progress from just winter camping to climbing mountains in winter. So we worked on some 14ers for several years. On several of them, we would just ski up and camp at tree line, 11,000 feet on the first day. Then on day two, we would scramble up the rocky windblown icy slopes to the top in big down coats and mittens. I still had the snowmobile boots though!

On Longs Peak, we decided to climb Meeker first and traverse over.

Problem was it was too deep and steep to ski, so we plugged and post-holed all the way up in thigh high snow. Finally, reaching the rocky windblown ridgeline and the summit of Mt. Meeker, we turned back before dark. I would not climb Longs Peak until later. When I climbed it in the future, it was with Terry and Dave, and we used our hands and feet and a rope on a cliff. I will never forget hiking off that mountain in complete darkness. Another story.

I knew I needed more experience and the next step would be more altitude.

So, I set off and climbed the Mexico volcanoes. At 20,000 feet, I felt my first altitude sickness debilitate me into a slump on the slopes. Weakness and fatigue were so relentless, I turned back just before the summit of Ixtapa. It's best not to fly in and climb right up the next day. Climbing Orizaba, the next few days, was a success.

I kept up with my backcountry travels forever it seemed. Slap on a heavy pack and skis and head for a peak. Leaving at 6 p.m. on a full moon with just my dog, I would ski up Ripple Creek Pass arriving after midnight, throw out some pine branches and make a nest for the night cuddled with my Jenny. We would both shiver and be restless for a while but finally, settle into a comfortable sleep after watching the bright full moon traverse the sky with the dark shadows from the tall pines dancing in the windy night. It was bliss.

Or ski the ten miles up to Conundrum Hot Springs, arriving at dark and sit at 11,000 feet in a rocky hot pool till midnight. Then sleep in the snow. Bliss! Then climb Conundrum Peak the next day. Bliss! One trip up there, I missed my buddy who had skied up before me, and I just kept skiing in the dark, Gibbous moon and all. It had been a long trip due to the recent avalanches that had strewn the path with huge trees and piles of snow. I ended up above the tree line before I figured out where I was. I just made camp there and found him the next day. I was among the high peaks, towering above me. They were covered in snow, except the rocky bands of contrast that stretched down the valley below. Oh my God, the stars. I was in the throne room of the mountain gods. Bliss!

Or throw on those skis and grab Gary and ski hard all day with packs, camp in the snow 13 miles later. Tents were too heavy.

Then with lightened packs, ski up the ridgeline above the Lost Lakes in the Flattop Wilderness area attempting to ski to the top of the flat tops. Oh, the view is bliss.

Do it all again in a month except a new peak, Sand Point on the Little Flat Tops where we found a bear den in the snow. Or my favorite was with Dave and Dennis and a two-day ski to climb Pyramid Peak. A special time in my life's journey and a special place in my heart; the Williams Fork Valley, where I live surrounded by the flat tops.

"To be near something beautiful or precious but to be unable to experience it is the subtlest positive form of torture."

We all have those times when a flower loses its color for some reason, or the music no longer stirs us. Clouds can form, and the light can dissipate. This is what I felt after becoming so proficient at downhill skiing. Black diamond slopes no longer even appealed to me.

Clouds can clear, and the spirit can be refreshed. When I put on a pair of cross-country skis, a whole new world opened up. So many places to see. The exhilaration of traversing Rabbit Ears Pass on a full moon night, and 11 miles later, standing on top of the ski slope, alone, was refreshing my spirit. The beer at the bottom tasted so much better.

I loved skiing so much that I wanted to share it with others. I started a small guide service. Back in the '70s, a person had to ski into the Strawberry Hot Springs, and it was special for some people to experience the ski and a prepared dinner in a small wooden hut. Or a moonlit ski around Black Mountain. I would pack the trail. Or a winter camping trip to learn about the use of avalanche beacons and snow caving. I was in the service of others to show the way into back country travel sharing my love of the sport.

I shared this love with my boys and they skied at an early age. Their first winter camping trip was at the age of eight, and after a few miles, we camped below a small flow of ice where they got their first lesson in climbing frozen water. Terry was great at consoling their fears. The boys, Jake and Matt, experienced skiing, ice and rock climbing, canyoneering, biking, and running rivers all at an early age.

There were so many times I slept in the snow, but I must tell you about the teepee. Several friends and I built it at the base of Cyclone Park which lies on the slopes of the Beaver Flat Tops near my home now. We needed a base so we could ski up the open slopes above and then ski down them, all day long. Powder, powder, powder, weekend after weekend. Heavy packs for only three miles and then the freedom of just your skis. It was hard panting work to re-climb the hill time and time again. It was a drug and addicting.

Many friends came and visited the teepee, good times by all. Terry and I spent many a New Year's Eve at this spot. It was special. When I was skiing, I felt a greater freedom as my authentic self, solidified in a wholeness I can't explain. I felt this later in my mountaineering exploits. But sometimes dreams unwind. Like in the mountains, clouds can drop and leave your dreams in a foggy white blanket, like climbing Everest.

Backcountry traveler.

Heading up to teepee to Ski Cyclone Park.

II

The 1996 Everest climb was written up as a deadly disaster. In many books after and after several movies produced, it was portrayed as the 'disaster on Everest'.

In all the magazine stories, it was a disaster.

Before the disaster, it was still a famous climb because of other reasons. We had one of the first satellite phones ever to be used on an Everest climb and that enabled one of the climbers to keep in contact with NBC news as to the progress of the first American woman to climb Everest. Tom Brokaw would give updates on our progress. Reporters were on a trek with us to base camp. Jon Krakauer from *Outside Magazine* was on the New Zealand team. Jon was supposed to be on our team, but at the last minute, he joined the Zealanders. IMAX had a film crew on a separate team and was just going to film the climb of Everest by Ed Viesturs. But that all changed when the disaster happened and the story changed. Ed and Scott had summited K-2 together.

A lot of people were trying to do 'first' Everest events. First women by a certain country, Norway, Japan, America, etc. First major film, personal firsts, some country's first time, a country's first solo. I ponder now at this stage of my life, 68 years old, and wonder what mental processes have changed in my adventure calculations, if any.

*

I reflect on my journeys that brought me into so many crazy situations, and I realize that I was trying to face my greatest fears. I was afraid of heights; I was afraid of water. So I would attack my fears with ferocity. Boatmen would avoid big holes in the river, and I would kayak into them. People were calling me crazy; one friend said I had a death wish. I think it was more like 'I want to live' wish. Proficiency and skills lead to confidence, and then one must work within one's limits. It's imperative to know one's limits.

I think I knew those limits when I set out to kayak Cross Mountain Gorge solo and made the first solo run. I think I knew those limits on Everest when I decided to turn back off the mountain.

"Seek your friends with time to live, not with time to kill," Shaw.

*

Tit for Tat

*"The world reposes in beauty to he who walks serenely on a path without secret violence,
As he who sails the river, resting his bark in the calm and carrying it around the cataracts."*

Henry David Thoreau

A person can sit by the river yearning and learning, every movement of the water can make a person contemplate whatever he wants. The water teaches you reflection. The attraction here is obvious, and the adventure is plentiful. This was and still is a passion in my life. For 45 years now, I have seen the flow of cataracts and tranquility of rivers from Costa Rica to Alaska. Mini expeditions into beautiful canyons and cliffs.

Grizzly bear tracks are seen along the banks of the river. Ambling footprints of great size. The Tatshenshini River flows from Canada's Yukon territory to Dry Day, Alaska. Grizzly, black, moose, lynx, caribou, wolves, peregrine falcons, and bald eagles can be seen here. An abundance of wildlife along a fourteen-day expedition with a forceful river that carves through the highest and most spectacular snow-covered mountain ranges and you have a spectacular but risky adventure. Back in the mid '70s, it had just been rafted for the first time. I had to do it. I would have to say after all the river trips I have done, this was the most spectacular!

*

Many years before, Dave Mondeau got me into rafting and

showed me the ropes. I have been on so many trips with Dave. At that time, I had to buy three old Udisco boats for cheap in order to get people to go with me. I was not going to be on any guided trip. People were not hard to find for sharing in the adventures. Back then it was not so crowded on the rivers; permits were easy to get. Now everyone seems to have a boat. Having trained people to run my boats, it allowed me to kayak. To really get in touch with the feel of the river. Graz, Dennis, Dave, Tom, Ed; many others were boatmen to carry the loads and share the fun.

*

The Tatshenshini River, aka the Tat, is so remote, so spectacular, and so grand. For 14 days, we float in rafts down a silty river through a land of towering peaks and views of untouched glaciated mountains, valleys, and ice fields to the largest non-polar ice glacier in the world. Off in the distance is the highest coastal mountain, Saint Elias. It is truly an expedition in rafting.

Haul your gear up to Washington State, put it on a ferry to Haines, Alaska, build oar frames and kitchen boxes, hire a truck to take you to the put in, hire a few small planes to pick you up at the ocean. Then reverse the process to get you home. We made it happen.

*

Don't get me wrong; the Grand Canyon is also a special place to enjoy. I have spent much time there, playing in deep thrashing holes of liquid turmoil in my kayak. Terry and I would feel the anxious grip when scouting Lava Falls. We often joke now about how her kayak would run the rapids better without her in it. She can tell you stories about swimming every rapid in the Grand. I would kayak the fast-flowing turmoil and deep holes of Lava and hike up and run it again in the rafts.

On one trip through, the raft flipped, and I was washed up against a large rock on the bank. The water was just flowing over it, banging me around, while still holding my breath. On the backside was a whirlpool that sucked me down so violently, I was spinning and felt the pull to the river bottom. It would spit me out, and as I surfaced it, would grab me again and pull me down. I was holding my breath the whole time about ready to suck in water. It had sucked my wetsuit booties right off my feet! I finally made it to shore, but my eardrum had been blown out due to the rapid changes in depth in the whirlpool. My ear began to dribble out blood and I was in intense pain. It felt as though my head was going to burst. I seriously knelt there in the sand holding my head while looking for a cliff to jump off of in order to stop the pain. I did not want this torture to last any longer.

Seriously, I wanted to jump. I started popping codeine pills and took so many, it put me in a coma. I guess it was a coma, I was out for days. They loaded me on the back of a raft and I slightly remember holding on to the baggage while running other rapids. Am I crazy?

I ran many other Grand Canyon trips after that. It was fun to be rowing with my sons, Jake and Matt, on many trips to come. They have already run it more times than I have.

*

At the put-in of the tat, we tried stacking our cases of beer in a tall column. We could not do it. Too many, too tall; it would fall. I lagged behind at the put in to clean up. When I kayaked down, the team had already entered 'No Turn Back Canyon'. A fast-flowing small river at this point. A continuous rocky rapid with fallen trees lining the river bank. Here we were in one of the largest wilderness areas of the world alone. The first raft proceeded to rip a tube open about three feet long. We made camp with grizzly tracks everywhere. Expedition style, we slept with our shotguns at hand. We sewed up the tear and placed a big patch. The next day, we lost a kayak in the rocky rapids and a good camera. Expedition style we moved on to bigger things. River and mountains.

*

I was a very proficient kayaker, lending rescue to others and flipped rafts all the time, over the many years. I enjoyed the time with my good friend Ed or Edward or Ed-brella. He is no longer with us. Old age gets us one way or the other. I miss him. When the bald eagles fly, I still remember him the most.

Ed was just learning kayaking at the time I took him down

Cataract Canyon on the mighty Colorado River. He got a big first look at rescue. The boatmen flipped the first two boats in big drop two, also called Little Niagara. This is the only time my eighteen-foot Rogue raft has ever flipped. Even with multiple trips down the Grand Canyon, the Rogue had never flipped.

Watching this unfold on shore, I commanded Graz and Tom to get going and hope for the best with their raft. We must all help with the rescue. The worst rapid was just below and all passengers from the flipped rafts were now swimming in it; Big Drop Three, aka Satan's Gut.

Ed must have been having second thoughts at the time in his new kayaking adventure. But he had this tenacious adventuresome spirit like no other.

We punched the hole in Niagara and paddled at the top of the big drop. I remember telling him that we had to go for it without a scout. People were swimming in it. A pregnant woman to boot. The rapid is gnarly to say the least, but kayakers have the ability for self-rescue, the roll. We punched our way through the spray and dived into holes and were thrown sideways in an instant with the waves.

Tom and Graz did just fine and helped with the rescue. With our kayaks, we pulled swimmers to shore or over to Graz. Then for miles, we rescued the two flipped boats and various gear. When all were safe, a party with many stories then ensued. Gary rescued his pregnant wife; Dianna swam under a boat and got to shore, walking for miles downstream over boulders to catch the team. Karen and Cacy somehow got on top of the flipped raft. Jamie swam through the holes holding her breath. Cooper held onto the raft while swimming the big drop. Nadine got caught under the boat. We ran it again years later. Another story.

*

The Tat grows bigger very fast, a huge river with glacial melt. Rocks can be heard rolling downstream below you. It's swift for such a large river.

Many tributaries are rushing in all the time. You can see the rocks caving in from the banks, ever changing the landscape. The water is icy cold. Don't swim here.

They say that big mountains and big rivers attract big spirited people. I feel blessed to have found the right people. It's just amazing to experience one of the most untouched areas of wilderness in the world with good friends and Terry was one of them. We pass a rapid called Lava North. It just appears out of nowhere. A huge hole in the middle that was a raft flipper. Don't swim here; the river is too wide, and you would be frozen by the time you reached shore. An icy cold-water swim is deadly. I have had convulsive shakes from winter time swims on other rivers.

The warmest rivers I ran was with Ed and Linda in Costa Rica. It could be raining on you while you slept in a puddle of water and still be warm. We were invited on a guided trip. All the people were very experienced guides and owned raft companies. It was an expedition to run three rivers and to entice people to come to run rivers there. We were experienced tagalongs. It was also going to be a trip to help save the Pacuare River that was planned to be dammed soon. Ed and I were kayaking a class IV-V river in warm water. It was wonderful. Rapids with the consequences of 'go left' and die were common.

Large white birds dotted the sky above the forest jungle. We scouted the rapids at every turn. For days this went on, sleeping with poisonous frogs. On my travels, I got to see Lava falls, Lava North, and now on the Rio Chirripo, I got to see Lava South. Another huge rapid with relentless power and one big death trap of a hole. Seems you could not see down to the bottom of it, but I digress.

*

The Tat is actually one of the most heavily populated corridors for Grizzlies in Canada. It was always on our mind and we were constantly searching for a sighting. We had climbed a peak with guns and after the sun went down, we slept for an hour and then the sun was up again. In one hour, no bears, thank God!

*

Overall rafting fast rivers present a greater adventure. Fast water makes for bigger rapids and less thinking time for maneuvering. Flood stage. On the middle fork of the Salmon, we took the risk of going down the canyon in such a state. Our trip leader had had enough of big water and did not show up. We made the trip anyway and found the river running over its bank and the liquid flush was rushing through the trees. It was the first time that I was on a trip with Jake and Matt, my sons, each oaring a separate boat. Memorable.

*

Also, it's not so much the solitude that makes the trip so remarkable as it is the scenery. A fast-flowing large river among high peaks was the prelude to the crescendo the orchestra plays as we oared into the epic beauty of Alsek Bay. The Tat combines with and turns into the Alsek River. We camped across from the glacier that stood with 300-foot-tall cliffs of ice. Icebergs floated calmly in the bay. The land of the midnight sun. Towering snow-covered peaks. It takes your breath away, renders you speechless, and all that you can do shake your head in disbelief and drop your jaw.

*

Rapids can drop your jaw. In both 1983 and 1984, we had record snowfall and the Yampa River was at a 100-year flood stage. So, away we go, down the Yampa. The river was running through the put-in, campground, and picnic tables; all were nearly underwater. I have run the Yampa many, many times but to see Warm Springs rapid at this level was historic. It has two holes at the top and one massive river wide hole at the bottom. It was exploding with a curl back wave that shot water back into the air as it crashed down on itself.

In slower years, I would kayak and run the top two holes just for play before quickly maneuvering out of the way of the last big hole. Just tempting my fate as it were. Playing.

This year even the boatmen on the trip did not want to run the rapid. I ran close to the bank on the river right with my kayak and it was tough. A large boat was way less maneuverable. I walked back up and took the next raft through, one of the only times I wore a helmet when in a raft. I totally expected to flip. Trips before us reported flipping four out of five boats. That was common for a couple of weeks. The river was running 34,000 cubic feet of water per second in a tight narrow slot next to the canyon wall. Thank God, to this day, I have never flipped a raft. So much campfire fodder.

Warm Springs rapid, Yampa River. 100-year flood stage, 34,000 cfs.

*

The Tat combines with the huge Alsek River and we camped across the bay from the Alsek Glacier about a mile away. A lot of driftwood was on the beach. We could hear a crash as the glacier calves off another iceberg. Then this sound of more crashing. One after another after another. I kept saying, "Listen!" at which time campfire talk would subside temporarily. It was getting closer. Then the wave hit! All our gear, cameras, coolers were sunk or afloat. The sound we had repeatedly heard was from the wave hitting other icebergs in the bay for a whole mile as it worked its way toward 'unsavvy' rafters who had set up camp below the driftwood line! Duh! Our rafts were pushed up on shore and had to be lugged back to the water, but Alsek Bay was not through with us yet. The next day, while trying to make the pull, I was watching an eagle swoop down on a bird on shore. I consequently missed the pull into the main river current and was soon being sucked into an enormous back eddy, which would have led us around the wrong side of the island. That direction would have swirled us among a graveyard of icebergs, any number of which might have sandwiched us or possibly flipped the boat.

As I neared the opposite bank, I screamed, "Jump," at Terry, which she dutifully did holding the coiled bowline in her hands. The rope was running through her hand inch by inch, burning flesh. She had to hold us on shore while the powerful back eddy pulled the boat further and further into it. She dug in with her feet like a game of tug-of-war with an 18-foot raft! I can't tell you the screaming and yelling that was going on at that moment, but it wasn't pretty. Help arrived and on we went.

The last day, we floated out in a mile-wide river running fast and deep and with icebergs bobbing down the river. Sometimes, they would grind to a stop on the river floor and make for a dangerous blue obstacle. You had to be alert.

Alas, our last day, and we were out of food. So it was good to arrive at the fishing camp. At Dry Bay, near the ocean, we burned the oar frames we had built along with the wooden boxes. Those heavy wooden items would be too heavy for the weight limit in the small planes we had hired to fly back.

The plane flight out was the last phenomenal symphony. Gliding over the river that passes close to the highest peaks on the continent, we stretch our necks to view the eye candy of stunning glaciers, braided streams, flowers and our very first grizzly bear sighting along the beach. Snow-capped peaks seem to stretch forever as did the route we had just floated.

Alsek Bay.

Alsek River, Alaska, ice chunks floating behind boat (Karen).

Highest coastal mountain range in the world. Mile wide Alsek River with icebergs bobbing along.

Crystal Rapid in the Grand Canyon

III

After the long trek up the valley with porters and yaks, the expedition finally arrived at Everest base camp. Scott was always tending to business with the sherpas, other teams, and clients. He was so wrongly depicted in the movie *Into Thin Air,* as arrogant and laid back. This was not the guy I knew. Sure he felt as an equal to the best climbers in the world at the time, but he took care of business. He was accommodating and kind. He had a good nature about him.

Base camp is a captivating, breathtaking, grand aurous sight. Right before your eyes, the massive mountains on all sides jet up to the sky with glaciers carving and tumbling off the cliffs. Periodic avalanches cloud the sky in angelic white dust. The brightest blue sky imaginable is overhead and the clouds can be seen, drifting ever higher up from the valley below. It seems like a person could step right off the glacier and glide right on top of the delicate puffs of elegantwhite. This was home for the next month.

Walk from snow to the top of the clouds.

The Khumbu Glacier is the ground upon which we camp and sleep and the glacier above falls off a cliff and forms a tumbling mass of ice towers called seracs. These can collapse suddenly and crevasses can open up with little warning. Huge blocks of ice can tumble down from time to time; their sizes can vary from car size to house size. A delicate flow of frozen water, moving as much as a meter in a day.

This is where we must go on our first trip up. The Khumbu Ice Falls, the longer you are in, the better chance you have at being buried alive. You can hear it collapsing and cracking; stuff comes down every day. In 2014, sixteen sherpas lost their lives here. Excitement with a cautious enticing allure runs through my body.

In Ouray Colorado, I smashed my fist into the ice,

unfortunately as hard as I could. My knuckles revolted in pain. The ice axe held nicely though. It was just bad technique on my part. One bad placement, and it would be a bad fall. That was the way it was, always, with ice climbing. There could be no mistakes. Every foot kick and hold, every pick placement was critical all the time. If you were a lead climber, that was how you had to roll. This was my first lead. I kicked and climbed another step.

Dave Mondeau had taught me the ropes for years and he was only equaled by Scott Fisher, both my very good friends. I spent years climbing ice with Dave and Scott in Ouray, Colorado, and Canada; as well as Nepal and Pakistan, I climbed another kick and placed my axe more angled this time so as not to bang my knuckles again. We were up about a rope length, 100 feet or more. Dave was belaying me from an ice ledge a few feet wide and had himself pinned into the wall of a frozen waterfall. Releasing one arm, it meant that my other arm was the only thing preventing my fall. You think a lot about an ice axe placement at that time. Your forearms start to burn with fatigue if you stay too long in one position. You must keep moving. It's as if you stress out your one muscle till it's at its fatigue point, then switch to the other arm muscle. I stepped up. Each leg movement is the same. You are standing on two little prongs at the front of your boots. Stand too long and your leg starts to shake. I move up but start to feel my axe slip.

*

Scott gave clinics every year on New Year's Eve, and Dave and I would go and help out. Eventually, Terry would, too. Eventually, I was leading clients. Dave led me up all the falls in Ouray and then I was able to take Terry up the same. Several trips to Canada with Scott, Terry, and I climbed most of the falls there. Terry even led some ice there.

*

My axe did not break loose, but the feeling of losing it still makes my heart race. Sometimes, your pick is only a few inches in, but you have to trust it anyway. You have to move. The second pitch we were on was only 30 ft high, but it was dead vertical. Not undulating or cascading. There is a real difficulty in placing an ice screw in for protection on vertical ice. One arm is all you have to hold onto while you frantically try to hammer in a pin.

Sometimes, it's not worth the risk to stop and burn out your arm. So, you proceed without protection. Halfway up the pitch my arms were burning.

*

I have so many memorable climbs, each a story, but the one I feel the most passionate about is with Terry at Gibraltar Wall in Canada. The reason is that it was in such a remote area of the country. Nobody was around and we were in solitude. We would have no rescues at this spot.

There were no cell phones back then. It was a three-pitch climb and the center section was steep with questionable chandelier ice; not well frozen. I led the first pitch which was jolly and laid back, very fun. It did, however, gain altitude fast and we pinned in on a gentle ledge with death- defying exposure.

The second pitch was the crux, and it was steep. The ice would break off easily, and icicles would come crashing down. The lead climber must be offset from the belayer. That way, the falling masses of water in the frozen form will not hit Terry below! Sometimes, you must punch away a lot of ice in order to find good ice. It is so much harder to find a solid pick placement. It was very strenuous, but our experience by this time was solid. We had become well versed and were a good team. The next belay spot I pinned in and hung there while Terry climbed it in fine style.

She led the final pitch across the slope in a traverse to the rappel spot. What a scary, high and exposed spot it was. Rock at the very top made it difficult to climb through. What a view.

Near the top of my very first lead ever, I was breathing hard. Arms were burning, legs were okay. It's important to know your strength and to know your limits. To know what you can and cannot do. This comes with a lot of practice. Confidence is a must. There are always surprises though. There was a lip at the top of the falls. The ice lays back and it's flat on top. One might think that's easy to just step up on it, but it's not.

At this point my knuckles had taken a few more smashes, and I'm breathing very hard as my muscles require a lot of oxygen. Of course, the forearms are burning, but these are the expected parameters that you know you have to work within. The confidence still remained high. If you lose your confidence and you panic, then things go to hell. That all can happen within seconds.

*

I had reached a high level of confidence later in my climbs and one day, when Scott and the others gave up for the day, I went climbing solo. They had to quit due to falling ice. It was warm and the falls were coming apart. Very dangerous if you are at the place where gravity places you beneath objects. I picked a climb called Horsetail Falls in a gorge that remained in the shade and stayed colder. I had led it before placing protection at certain levels and knew it well. Climbing solo, there is no protection, no rope, no rescue. Just pure solitude and three cascading pitches of monolithic frozen blue waterfalls. I can't explain the exhilaration of being alone in the middle of the falls, hanging there by your arms with only ice above and ice below. I carried a rope on my back for the awesome rappels down.

*

Meanwhile, back to my first lead climb. I reached over the lip and placed the picks one by one as far into the flat ice at the top. I step up and up. Now my body is bent over with my butt in the air. I can't quite step up on the lip yet. I can't put my knee down; it would just slip right off. How terribly awkward this was. My legs were now in the shaking mode from fatigue from such a bent over position. They call this a sewing machine knee. I had to move. It was snowing and now my hands were frozen.

So, the frozen hands were not a concern. The flat lip and step up was a concern. I reset the axes and I just pulled myself up with arms only, feet dangling, holding with one arm and resetting one pick. Then pulling up and resetting again. Like

47

pull-ups. Dave made it look easier. Dave always made it look easy. Dave would always say in his calm demeanor, "Good job, Dale."

They say you never forget your first, and I certainly will not.

*

Frozen hands, cold feet, snowing and wet clothing, spindrift avalanches, falling ice, hanging out on cliffs, yea what great fun it was. At the end of all the climbing days, we would drink and Scott would tell his stories about climbing K-2 or Everest or any of the many. We were pumped on natural spices of the primordial soup. We would laugh at many things but never a complaint about the conditions. It was part of the aura, the allure, the fascination. We were climbers. I met some of the best climbers in the world when I was with Dave and Scott. In the back of my mind was always the possibility of climbing Everest myself. Maybe, doubtfully, maybe though.

I was happy to be in the right company. Climbing with Terry was special. Who else would follow me around vertically?

Terry following me vertically.

IV

On the Khumbu icefalls of Everest, we had only one small vertical section and the rest was hiking and climbing around ice chunks, skirting crevasses, and walking across ladders over crevasses. The team was getting ready and the sherpas were already on their way with loads to Camp I. I moved ahead and soon found myself way ahead of the group. I did not see anything I had not experienced before and felt comfortable, confident, and strong. I knew that many of the other climbers did not have the experience that I had in ice climbing and Scott and the guides, Neal and Anatoli, moved along with them. They were all adept with these conditions anyway.

I came to a crevasse that was so big you could drive a whole freight train into it and not see it anymore. I stood alone at the edge and admired the force of nature. Somewhere down there, water was running and lubricating the glacier allowing its faster movement down the valley. I wondered what it would be like to be down there, impossible to get out, the walls too vertical and undercut to climb.

In front of me were three aluminum ladders tied end to end laid flat over the crevasse. One rope ran above it about three feet higher. The ladder at my end was tied in with ice screws. I clipped into the rope with my carabiner and stepped onto the ladder, balancing one step at a time, one ladder rung at a time. My crampons had to hit just right on the rung so as not to trip me up. I felt like an elephant with spike shoes and my trunk was holding me to the safety rope. The ladder bending down with my overabundant weight. At the first joint of the ladder, I checked out the lashings that tied the ladders together and praised the work of the Sherpa that created the knots.

I moved on and through more seracs and shorter ladders and some vertical ladders. I cross snow bridges that would later melt out and expose a crevasse below. Twirling twisted cornices created caves ending in a dark unseen place. After many hours, I came to a crevasse that had to be crossed and found a six-foot-wide snow bridge that provided a good route. I stepped gently forward and sighed in relief on the other side.

I waited at Camp I for about an hour and then headed down. Scott was moving ahead of the group and he was happy to see me; I suppose relieved that I was okay and I think impressed I had taken the initiative to move through the falls on my own. We enjoyed a cup of tea next to the crevasse. It was here they would set a record for altitude helicopter flight on Everest and make several rescues in a couple of weeks.

Freight trains parked below.
(Photo by Neil Bieldelman)

*

Fears

So what about fears? What causes us to not be so fearful. What makes us at other times feel panic. In my primordial soup, I think back.

I guess we try to calculate our adventures by looking at our fears of the impending risk. Our fears may just be too high to take the risk. The fear is the safety rope that pulls us back into a comfortable place.

My fears of tight spaces stayed with me from the first time I volunteered to take a class of junior high children into Spring Cave near Meeker, Colorado. Mike Frazier was leading the group and knew all the passages very well. He led us through the tight spaces and we were crawling one at a time through the narrows. Everyone carried two flashlights, and it was a train of chaotic echoing voices like in a scary movie. We came to the Butterscotch Room, and we could all fit in the low roof cavern. Mike slithered into a hole in the floor and said, "Follow me."

I did. I was now in a room as small as a closet. He instructed me to 'wait here' and help the others through in the right direction. He then slithered down another hole. As the children came, it turned into a bottleneck and several kids were joining me in this tight space. No one was going anywhere. Dark, tight space, flashlights only, too many people in one place. Claustrophobia. Fear rising, but nowhere to escape it. Panic, I was starting to feel the rise of my loss of control. It rises and you must force it back down. It is tough to do. Think, breathe, relax.

The same thing happened to me in another cave, except we had scuba tanks on and were under 40 ft. of water. Terry, Linda, Ed, and I swam into the Bear's Den on the Honduras Coast. It had been closed to commercial diving because people had panicked there and died. There is a small room you must enter and then flatten out and swim into a passageway into the larger room. The roof of the passage is just a few feet off a sandy bottom. There is light that shoots through holes in the roof in the small room, creating a magical aura of rays and spotlights, especially when you turn off your flashlights. A bewitching and elegant place.

In the small room, there was a bottleneck and the previous swimmer had kicked up a bunch of sand, creating a cloud that you could not see through. Plus, the opening was so tight it would all be just a swirl of sand. I drifted upward and looked closely at the tight hole with the light penetrating through above me. Fear is rising up inside me. I knew this is how people had died, trying to fit through the hole and swim into the light, then getting stuck as even more panic would set in. Breathe, think, relax, wait. The sand will clear. It did.

Fear can also be a safety rope, but peer pressure can push you into situations you would rather not be in. Terry and Linda and Ed wanted to dive with sharks without a cage. I did not, but I succumbed to peer pressure or wife pressure.

The boat led us to a far-out buoy that the guides had set up just for the purpose of taking clients to the reef below. The current was so strong here that we had to hold on to a cable that was anchored below. If you missed the cable, you would be swept away, and they joked that they would pick you up in Panama. Scary with all the sharks below.

We dove down to the reef below all in a line and backed

up to a rocky reef below. A few sharks and that was intense enough, but then the guide started pulling out bloody fish to chum the sharks. As she placed a fish as far out as she could, the smaller fish from around the reef would attack it with a ball of frenzy. Twenty, thirty small fish all trying to get a bite. Then the sharks moved in fast. One, two, five, so fast and attacking with incredible speed. Taking a bite out of anything in their way. Then it was calm and they were just coursing back and forth over and around the reef.

Then the guide swam out about six feet and tried to throw the fish in front of her while swimming backward. A shark swam straight for her fins and pulled back within inches, making a ninety degree turn in a flash. My heart was pumping now as more than ten sharks were buzzing all around. How were we going to get out of here? Fear rising, breathe, relax, wait. We later swam up the cable as sharks circled below in a threatening way. My eyes were wide open all the time. Attacking our fears, it's just the spice the soup needs to evolve.

V

At Camp II on Everest.

We placed the Sherpa in our Gamow bag after he struggled not to go into it for a while. The bag can be pressurized by a foot pump and can increase the available oxygen to the occupant. However, he was suffering from pulmonary edema, and the fluid in his lungs was already severe. He was also an older gentleman and that did not serve him well. Sherpa of that age were known to be smokers their entire lifetimes. They said it gave them energy. With any edema, it is very important to lose altitude as fast as possible, if possible.

Klive was one of the strongest members on our team and he helped the other Sherpa carry and drag him down the cwm and the ice falls. An amazing feat crossing those ladders.

At base camp, they continued with the Gamow bag, and the camp doctor on our team treated him as best she could. He needed to go lower yet. In the following week, she and others helped him down the glacier and the valley, but other heart problems started to occur. He was finally hospitalized in Kathmandu and spent a month there before he died.

While climbing the next few weeks, I truly thought he would be okay.

In my continuing search of motivation for serious adventures, I need to put rock climbing as the biggest boost in gaining experience in mountaineering. I did not want to be just a peak bagger, but someone who climbed the peak with style. Whether it was with skis, on rock, or on ice. I had a fear of heights, but that soon went away. In a quest for mountaineering skills, I needed rope work.

Again, it was Dave Mondeau who taught me the ropes. He was already a climber by the time I met him and had done routes with Scott Fischer in various places. Dave led me up cracks and cliffs and made it really fun. He would take me to Moab and we would do our thing in the heat of the desert. There were few people climbing back then in the early eighties.

Rarely did you see many other climbers. If you did, they were probably putting up first assents for rock routes or unclimbed spires. Now it's so packed with climbers you can't find a place to park.

Dave made the first ascent of the Monitor and the Merrimack! They are two large, wide chunks of rock that are prominent monolithic features in Moab. That's how unclimbed things were back then. The eighties. Mountain bikes had not been invented yet. Telephone booths were abundant.

Dave took me on my first multi-pitch climb on a cliff, a wall. We were going to be the first to climb the Warlock Spire in Moab. Aid climbing was a big thing back then. Place a chalk in a crack above you, then hook your rope ladder and step up. Although you always used your hands and feet if your ability allowed. With vertical walls, it was rarely free climbed, at that time. Things change; people are much better climbers now, and they often free climb.

It was thrilling to hang out on a rock wall 400 feet up and watch Dave climb above me. We were alone in the desert. Solitude. The desert floor ran out forever below us, broken only with other red spires of Wingate sandstone in the distance. Wow! Then, the top was even better, about the size of a living room with views 360 degrees. We rappelled down after fixing two pins to the rock to hold us. It was not over yet. We had to climb our fixed ropes back up another cliff where we had left ropes hanging.

A 'jumar' is a device you hook to a rope that clamps on. You slide one up and then the other while your feet are attached to the loops and to the jumar. You go straight up one foot at a time with heavy packs! Very strenuous. It was my first wall climb and my first, first ascent. We got our names in a book. I say this only to show the motivation that propels a climber to do even more. We did!

Lightning storms are not a good place to be while hanging from a rope. We could see the storm far off in the distant desert landscape. Lightning bolts are magnificent to watch from far away. One dark cell was moving ever so slowly across the plain. We were jumarring back up a cliff from a climb on Budro Butte. We knew we had to beat the storm and get off the cliff. Heavy packs of gear made for a slow go.

Close to the top, I heard my carabiner above me start to hum and then a shissst and spark. Then the intense loud crack and white light around me. My hair stood up, and to say I was startled is putting it mildly. My heart was pounding as I rushed onward, inches at a time. No rain just yet. But when we reached the top, we spread out from each other fast. We avoided the small juniper trees and though there were overhangs, we stayed clear.

Overhangs can be deadly if lightning is close enough. I guess it can fry you like a flash oven. We just stood their hundreds of feet apart in pouring rain and thunder.

The lightning storm at Echo Park in Dinosaur National Monument was the best one ever though. We had fixed ropes up a cliff about 300 feet on Steamboat Rock and on a four-foot-wide ledge, we made camp. It was a glorious view of the Green River below and of the tan cliff walls painted with black varnished streaks of Jenny Lind Rock on the other side. When the white streak appeared across the river, you could feel the sound a split second later. Oh, you could feel it, and hear it! And hear it, and hear it, and hear it, and hear it about ten times. The sound would bounce off Jenny Lind and back over to Steamboat Rock and back again over and over.

What a great place to be on a cliff, in a lightning storm, in Echo Park! Electrifying. Later, we also found a rock at the bottom of our ropes, down by the river the size of a Volkswagen. It had cratered in the ground and come from above somewhere.

Later in the climb, on the big monolithic wall of Steamboat Rock, the crack just stopped. We had to set a pin, rappel down a way, then start running across the face of the cliff and do a pendulum swing to reach another crack. It was just like kids on a playground, Nice.

We finally made the top after two weekends and five days hanging about on the cliff. At the top, we were able to add our names in an old film canister with only two other parties. In 1953, Gale Weeding, and 1965, Layton Kor. Two infamous climbing legends. It was humbling because I was not in their league at all. I had read all of Kor's books. He made so many first ascents, including the first ascent of the North Face of the Eiger. Clint Eastwood made a movie of it. Also, in some older books, another fellow named John Wesley Powell claimed to have climbed this rock.

I am calling this bunk, especially since he had only one arm.

*

Rappelling is scary at first but becomes very second nature after a while. It is a lot of fun. Not so bad if you rappel down just one rope length, 160 feet. But I found a cliff that we had to tie 13 climbing ropes together to get to the bottom. The grand overhang in the Yampa River Canyon. Of course, there would be some problems. Of course, I got Dave to go and Terry supplied moral support and photos.

The cliff slopes down for a while and then drops in on itself creating an overhang otherwise known as a free rappel. You do not touch the wall; you are just hanging in space, cliff above, a clear greenish river way below.

White canyon walls all around you, painted with dark tiger streaks. The river snakes through pinion trees along sandy beaches and stretches for miles with more undulating cliffs. No traces of mankind, but there was plenty of fresh air, blue skies, and warm sun.

Problems can occur; adventure can find you. I started out and found that there was so much weight with all the ropes tied together that I couldn't just fall or walk down the cliff. I had to pull myself down. I mean pull hard for at least half way down the cliff. When I came to my first knot, I had to stop and jumar around the knot. This meant I had to release my rappelling device from me completely and put it below the knot. Well, after four or five knots, the rappelling device gets hotter than hell. It is extremely important not to drop it when it is free. I just had to let it burn my fingers.

Finally, out in free rappel, I was about half way down when the rope started to unwind multiple twists all the way up. I felt like a wound-up rubber band, going round and round and faster and faster. I tried concentrating on a point of land in the distance and turned my head around fast, like a ballerina. That did not work. I was getting sick. This was an amusement park ride and the worst kind. I closed my eyes and rode it out as it reversed direction. Awwwk. This happened for each length of rope several times.

What a sick ride!

I was so happy to get down that I just dropped with relief into the river below. I forgot I had my $600 zoom lens camera in my pack. There would be no pics of Dave. I hoped Terry got some of me from up top. She was using Dave's camera, and when we were all done and packed up, we found no film in Dave's camera. Bummer.

For some of you, I will have to explain what film is all about, or telephone booths.

*

We had no problems climbing the Castleton Tower in Moab. It was a free climb and 400 summiteers made it before us. It was first climbed in 1961 by Layton Kor again. Today, over 15,000 people have ticked this one off their list.

Dave and I had absolutely no problems when we made the first and only ascent of the magnificent geologic feature known as the Gates of Lodore. You have to see it to believe it. The river in Browns Park meanders slowly through low hills and plains and then dramatically cuts through a mountain.

The millions of years of erosion have left solid red rock walls towering above the Green River below.

This trip was a trip to paradise. We floated a small raft down to the beachfront campsite with a calm pool at the bank's edge. Swimming and bathing after a hot day of climbing, looking at towering, huge, red vertical walls above. Watching Peregrine Falcons dive for songbirds and listening to their screech. Box Elder trees with fluorescent green leaves provided shade when needed. Bighorn sheep were not afraid to share their spot with us.

The climb was as usual; hot, tiring work. One overhang provided quite the exposure while hanging there, making the moves to overcome gravity.

After five days of setting ropes, we hit a wide ledge near the top. As wide as a car and it ran along the cliff face to the edge of the mountain. Amazing place to be. We hiked around it some distance and when it hit the mountainside, we scrambled to the top of the peak.

Many rappels later, we joined our friends who rafted down to pick us up. Then we floated and learned from the river for four days. Yearning for more paradise. Ladore means to be somewhere between adoration and love. I adore this place!

Gates of Lodore (first ascent), paradise.

Warlock Spire on left, first, first ascent. Moab, U.T.

Dave on re-ascent of Steamboat Rock. Third day up.

Castleton Tower, Moab, U.T.

Grand Overhang, Yampa River. 1200-foot rappel.

VI

.

At Camp II on Everest, we had believed that our Sherpa was on his way home and would be doing fine. We prepared for our climb to Camp III. A great meal was prepared in the cook tent and then we settled into our tents. I shared a tent with Scott, and we talked very little before turning in. We were tired as it was.

The storm that night left us with the tent roof on our face all night.

Flapping and rattling. The poles had held well, but they were just bent over in our face with the gale force winds. Not much sleep at all, but that morning we pressed on to higher limits. After slogging for an hour or so, the glacier ends or starts here at the base of a steep ice slope. The shoulders of Lhotse and Everest combine here to gain some serious altitude. It's a bluish ice that can be rippled with snow or melting ice creating a crunchy soft top layer at times. It is usually wind-blown. Here, at the base, I see yet another body frozen in time from some previous climb. It could have been years and years ago and the body finally exited the ice flow here or melted out.

*

Death is a disturbing occurrence in an adventure. You never expect it to happen; it just does. You find it disturbing and impactful. I have unfortunately witnessed my share of deadly loss on my travels.

I climbed with a friend, Ion Bolt, on a trip to Canada. He later lost his life climbing Foraker in Alaska. On my expeditions to peaks in Nepal, we crossed high passes that had the frozen remains of sherpas from previous crossings. On my climb in 1995 to Pakistan's Broad Peak, we were in the turmoil of a rescue on the nearby peak of K-2. Six people lost their lives, including the famous climber Alison Hargreaves.

Now on Everest, I walked past frozen bodies that had thawed out of the glacier from previous trips. In that year, 1996, one of the most dangerous tragedies on the mountain occurred. Fifteen people died due to the mountain's ferocity. This was the deadliest single year for the big mountain by 1996. I lost my good friend Scott.

I lost my climbing partner, Lopsang Sherpa, who I climbed with on Broad Peak and now Everest. He died later that fall in an avalanche on Everest. Anatolli Boukreev, also on our Everest trip, later died in an avalanche on Annapurna. Mountains are killers. A death zone.

Those accounts were just the people I knew or met. If you look at Everest overall, 300 people have died climbing there. In 2014, sixteen people died in an avalanche. In 2015, there was a large earthquake and at the base of Everest, a huge avalanche killed 19 people. Like an amusement ride to the top of the world, people wait in long lines to climb, and another 11 people died in 2019.

Jon wrote, *"Prior to 1996, one in four people died climbing Everest. In '96, one in seven died climbing Everest. So, it was a statistically safe year."*

Amazing, right? The only death-free year was 1977. In the death zone during a storm, there can be a reduction of 14% in oxygen uptake. The body cannot perform. Take a walk up a flight of stairs and tell me that your heart is not pumping fast. Now, imagine a heavy pack, on snow, and at altitude, all day, in a storm! When I was on the slopes, it was a snail's pace, one foot at a time and rest.

Due to the difficulties and dangers in bringing bodies down, most who die on the mountain remain where they fall. Wherever you go, there you are.

You can barely haul yourself much less another person. In 2015, I was interviewed by a New Zealand film crew that was headed to Everest to bring Scott's body down. They wanted some background interviews from me to include in their film. The earthquake in 2015 stopped all hopes. As a result of that earthquake, 9,000 people died in Nepal. It seems the mountain wants to keep its victims.

When you come to grips with death and you live through it, you have a scar. A wound that tries to heal, slowly, leaving its mark. You are affected. You are close to people, and then you are not. They are gone. A part of you goes with the person you lost. My run from Everest will be forthcoming.

Death comes in many ways. It's worse when you are close to its grip, right in front of you.

The Swing

I held her head in my hands, and she was breathing deep, gasping for air.

"Marsha, come on, stay with us, you're doing fine, hang in there," I would say over and over.

I quoted Ullman earlier about risks and well, I think I'm not so sure. Well, maybe, it's still true. There is no growth in what is safe and comfortable. We must move ahead, or maybe move not at all.

Marcia was not coaxed into going off the swing. Her free spirit led her up to that platform. I only wish I could have been up there with her to show her the way to reduce the risk. I walked out of the cabin and saw her sitting on the top platform, some thirty-feet high. She was smiling and funny. Jerry, her husband, came over about that time also. She must have been a very fun-loving person. She was anxious to show us a great time. When she left that platform, the swing seat dangled out from under her, and she was only supported by her arms grasping the rope. She gave it all she could to hold herself up.

Her breath became shallower and shallower for 20 minutes, then none at all. I gave her my breath for 40 minutes before the ambulance arrived and then ten to 20 minutes more. Her vomit was all wild raspberries and serviceberries. She must have been a real free spirit, must have enjoyed most anything. She died smiling and happy, she lived life full.

I hope we all live to be old, but maybe more importantly, I hope we all die smiling happily.

VII

24,000 Feet on Everest

The ice face to Camp III is steep and Anotoli had fixed a rope and secured it with ice screws so that we could climb with our jumar ascenders and packs. I was again ahead of the group and climbing well. Halfway up the ice, I lost my footing and slid down the slope until my carabineer caught me on the ice screw. Wow! I thought about the body below and said, "Thank you, Lord."

I believe it was Jon Krakauer that asked if I was okay and I moved forward, a bit embarrassed.

The Sherpa had already prepared the large tents we would all share at Camp III. I was feeling great but felt a bit tired as I waited for the others to show up. I had that 'feeling of relief' from accomplishing a good climb that day. I was now looking right up at the summit of Everest and it looked so close. So close. I was at 24,000 feet and Camp IV was only a short distance away. The slopes were wind-blown and looked formidable. Cold air was biting my core. It felt good to be mountaineering. Wholesome. I did not sleep well the night before in the wind. I fell asleep fast. A team member woke me and made me a cup of tea to rehydrate. I only had a few sips before I was out again. Out for the whole night and then some. Any longer here for me at this altitude and I would not be writing this story.

*

Feeling of Relief

What do old mountaineers do if they are still alive and want more thrills? They go sailing. Sailing is a fun and exciting lifestyle and an interesting mode of transporting oneself to new and lovely places. It is, however, not necessarily relaxing at all times.

The ocean is unforgiving and relentless in its pursuit of smashing things up. Things that happen to be your home. The ocean is broad and stretches on forever it seems. You are in total solitude and it's sometimes quiet and sometimes splashy and sometimes very, very bouncy with objects crashing around. It's the worry you feel all the time.

Am I safe? Can I make it to the next port? Will my anchor hold? Will we hit something?

To add to that fear, it is especially compounding when the boat breaks down when and where you don't want it to. This happened to us many times. Stress!

My wife, Terry, and I have had propellers break off, leaving us stranded and limping back to port. We have had heat exchangers break down and had to seek refuge before the nightfall. We have had fishing lines get tangled in the prop rendering it motionless. We have had an impeller go out and had to sail into a strong wind for days to reach a safe bay. We have had the dinghy escape from us many times, causing much stress. Thus, the name painted on its side 'Hou-dinghy' named after the famous escape artist Houdini.

One time, Hou-dinghy untied its knot and slipped away in

the dark when we were at anchor. Finally found with a spotlight, it was up against the cliff some 200 ft. away. I wanted to let it go till morning and not take any risk to rescue it. But my brave wife wouldn't have it. It would be gone with the tide by then. Terry swam out there in cold water and a sea of darkness and creatures. Humboldt squid are out at night!

Another time Hou-dinghy slipped away with a rising tide while we were walking down the beach. Slowly drifting out to sea but too fast for us to swim to it. That left us stranded on the beach and a long swim out to our yacht at anchor. We finally got it back. Stress and then feeling of relief.

We have had the water pump fail; leaving us un-maneuverable before the next big blow, which is the least desirable place to be in the Sea of Cortez. They say you can sail anywhere in the world if you can sail in the Sea of Cortez. The waves are steep and close together, unlike the Pacific where the waves are long and broad most of the time. The pump went out just after we had done a night crossing of 90 miles. The weather was good and we were now on the Baja peninsula, where there is no real help for a hundred miles. We had to make it back to the mainland before the next big blow. Stress!

We set full sails at dusk and had light winds that increased nicely into the morning. Night sailing can be stressful especially when the waves are rolling you back and forth hitting you on the beam. This happened a lot in our crossings. We sailed back through a tight spot between the cliffs at the harbor entrance around noon. I can't tell you the feeling of relief that we felt. These feelings of stress and relief were common experiences in our sailing career, but we kept doing it for some ten years.

Our biggest feeling of relief came after we spent a whole day in a big blow at anchor.

The Port of Escondido in the Sea of Cortez is a refuge for

boats behind a natural sea wall; thus, prohibiting the waves from entering. But the wind blows with ferocity in a northern blow. Usually 30 knot blows are common and you tend your boat and watch for the possibility of the anchor dragging. Many a sailor has had his anchor drag until it's just hanging in deep water, and he finds himself out to sea or smashed up against the rocks. Another big stress of sailing.

This blow was scary big and we knew it was coming. The radio talk was of 40 knot winds up the Baja. It was early morning, and Terry had to get the dog, Ali, to shore with the dinghy for dog toiletry stuff. I remained and set snubbers for the anchor chain. By the time she completed the dog walk, it was too late to get back to the boat safely. The big blow had begun fast, hard, and relentless. Already another boat had pulled from its anchor and had to motor to reset. A friend of ours had his dinghy roped up to the boat aft and the wind blew it over, motor and all. Terry hadn't noticed the wind acceleration on shore among the brushy landscape and had therefore taken too much time. It was too risky for her to get in the dinghy and return. It would have flipped her out at some point and there would be no rescue. She had a handheld radio, and we kept in contact. It's a time when you start making promises to yourself.

Like the time we got caught in a blow coming from the aft and the waves were building high and steep. The danger here lies in the fact that your boat has some speed and when the wave passes you, the boat wants to surf down the wave. We were surfing! If you surf too much, it will bury the bow in the wave below and spin and trash you about or capsize your vessel. I made a promise that I would shave my head if we got out of this one. And I did.

Anyway, back to the big blow.

Captains stood on their boats and watched as the wind

would catch the side of the boat and push it sideways one way and then hardback the other way. Like a huge pendulum weight attached to a thin thread of life. Tilting the boat over on its side each time. This went on all day. Boats were dragging and crashing into other boats. Some had to motor into the wind to keep from moving too much. One captain had opted for a motel room the night before not wanting to deal with the storm. He lost his boat.

Many other boats had to reset by taking the risk of pulling up anchor quickly, so as not to crash into something, then motor to a new spot and quickly drop anchor. When they did this, the wind would push their boats over to one side. Next, their boats would turn and then the wind would push them the other way violently. I monitored the radio and rescues were going on everywhere. Captains trying to help others re-stabilize boats.

My boat was not dragging. I was whipping around like a branch trying to stay attached to its lifeline. My snubbers to the anchor chain began to wear through from the constant thrashing back and forth. It happened so fast. I panicked for a second and raced to the set box for more rope. As I was making up new snubbers, I noticed the captain behind me looking quite worried, to say the least. He knew that if I broke loose, then I would hit and destroy his boat, and we would all be swimming somewhere. He was already pissed at me for anchoring too close to him. So, instead of just one snubber, I put on three which did the trick, thank God.

The winds had reached gale force by this time. This means that the wind is able to pick up water from the sea and blow it across the bay at you. It's 60 plus knots! What a great time it was with wind and water in your face while standing on the bow of your boat, watching your vessel sway and tilt, back and forth, 50 ft. at a time. Racing one direction and then back the other, all day long. Pendulum swing and swing all the while waves bouncing the boat.

Terry, watching from shore, wanted to make an attempt. Finally, as the wind died a bit later that afternoon, she went for it. There would be no rescue if the wind picked up the front of the dinghy and flipped her over. The small white cap waves in the bay would help that process immensely. She waited for a lull in the wind and made a slow calculated dash. I really held my breath for minutes as she approached. A flip would mean a swim with the water pushing her toward a concrete wall. There was no escape but to swim next to it until the dock, far down the bay. The dock was having its own problems. Ali, our dog, usually rode on the bow and her weight helped keep the bow down. However, one particularly large wave threw her back into Terry's lap, making things precarious at best. Terry quickly pushed Ali to the floor and motored on arriving safely, albeit, quite drenched.

The wind died later that night. That is what I mean by 'Feeling of relief'.

Calm before the blow.
See more below.

Promise kept.

*

*This above all; to thine own self be true, and it must follow,
as the night the day,
Thou canst not then be false to any man. Farewell, my
blessing season this in thee!*

Shakespeare.

Taking risks is a personal choice about how you want to live. You don't worry about living by someone else's standards or rules. You must live as your natural self. Without compromise, I needed to expand my learning of mountaineering like a monkey in a tree, picking up a stick and walking erect. The name 'Arrokoth' reflects the inspiration of looking to the skies and wondering about the stars and worlds beyond our own. I was looking for other mountains beyond my own little world.

*

I climbed Baruntse in 1991 with Dave. It had a knife ridgeline over a mile long and we had to traverse it to get to the 24,000-feet summit.

It was my first expedition experience in Nepal and Scott picked out one of the most remote valleys to gain access to this peak. It had only been climbed some four times before. I think we were the first Americans to do it.

We hired 150 porters to carry gear for a week to get there from Lukla.

They were incredible packers, overpasses with ice slopes, up steep valley trails, across glaciers, and frozen lakes. One fellow carried a crate that spanned from his knees to the back of his neck carrying over 50 dozen eggs. The rest carried the tents, food, bags, climbing gear, ropes, and stuff needed to climb for two to three weeks out of base camp. We had a team of ten climbers. The porters would usually only have on sandals because it's all they could afford. We paid them a dollar and fifty cents per day. After the strike, I think it was settled on three dollars. It was common practice at the time. Three dollars would have been a whole month's salary at the time. They would all sleep in large tents, all cuddled together to stay warm.

I have even seen some start a whole slope on fire, walking up the mountain with the flames.

After a week to get to base camp, they were all gone and we were left with only the cook crew and the liaison officer who spent the next few weeks in his tent staying warm.

On Baruntse, we had to fix ropes above our first camp on a steep slope of pure ice. Scott had set pins in the ice to hold a fixed rope. That way, the rest of us could jumar up with heavy packs to the next camp. We set up Camp II and rappelled down for more gear and to acclimatize. There were three lengths of rope on this pitch. But the screws were melting out of the ice.

It was not a good feeling to see screws responsible for holding you on the slope, only halfway in the ice. We reset the screws and packed snow on top to keep out the intense radiation exposure.

A couple of weeks later, Scott and Dave were on a summit bid, the first team. I was watching from base camp.

A vertical rock wall rises up from the valley floor thousands of feet and is capped with a white crown near the top a mile long. They had climbed the ice slope and traversed the back side of Baruntse to get to this knife ridge. I watched all day while two tiny dots made their way across the wind-swept fluted snow packed ridge to the summit. I wish I had a telescope.

Later, Scott told a story of how Dave was convinced that they were on the wrong side of the ridgeline. It had just seemed too steep to walk along the side of a slope with a 2,000 ft. cliff below you. One missed step and away you would slide, right over the cliff. Dave kept up his argument until Scott punched a hole in the upper side of the ice ridgeline and viewed another 3,000 ft. drop on the other side. That ended the argument.

On my summit attempt, we had a group meeting at Camp III just below an indescribable block of twisted snow cornices called the Opera House.

Twists and curves of wind-blown snow created caves with icicles. It was an amphitheater; so massive that you could hold a concert there. This was at the corner necessary to negotiate access to the knife ridgeline. Craig was in charge and asked each of the five climbers if we were ready. I replied in a Scott Fisher kind of way, "Let's go for a walk."

He replied with a yell, "This is no damn walk in the park."

I think he was as anxious about the climb as any of us, but we show it in different ways. Around the Opera House and on the ridge, it was different than what I expected. Two climbers turned around here. The sharp crest angles up to a far distant summit, but there were flutes along the way.

Imagine a blanket over the back of your chair and then crunch it up to form many wrinkles or waves in it. Also, tip the chair to one side, so it climbs up steeply.

We had to walk the ridgeline and also climb these flutes. And then rappel down them, on the way back. They were steep but not high. We used a lightweight water skier's rope anchored to a single snow stake at the top to rappel from.

Scary place, thinking of a crack starting in the snowfield, which would result in the entire slope sloughing out from under you. We were walking on an angle of more than forty- five degrees for a mile, up one slow step at a time. Punching holes in the deep snow. A week later, we celebrated our success in a small village, Dingboche, by playing the star bottle game.

The Bottle Game

On the way down the mountain, on most of our expeditions, it was a time of high emotions and levity. People felt really good. We would stop at a village and were served beer. Beer comes in a large Quart bottle, called Star Beer. Competition was thick and intense playing this game. Place two empty bottles on the floor and place your palms on top while grabbing the bottle. Then start moving the bottles one at a time in front of you. Keep your toes in one spot, they can't move. When you are horizontal and stable, without any part of your belly touching the floor, push one bottle out as far as you can with your fingertips. Furthest bottle out wins. It was always Dave, Scott, or I that had the thrill of success or the agony of defeat. The beer was good, too!

Some risks we encounter come to us beyond our control. The positive entropy of the universe. Movement toward disorder. We face these risks every time; we boil a pot of water or ride a bus.

After the Baruntse climb, we had trekked out to Lukla and waited in the storms at the cliff side airfield. Days and days went by after which Dave and I decided to hike out. Down the foothills

Baruntse, 24,000 ft.

4000-feet rock wall of Baruntse with knife ridgeline to the right, one mile long. (Dale, left, and Dave)

High camp, Baruntse. Opera House mid-slope with knife, ridgeline, along to summit.

Porters carry 3x what we do.

of the highest mountains, we traveled for days. I picked a few pot plants and dried them over my backpack for later use. We were left in awe with the sights and people we encountered in the isolated environment. Villages that sustained themselves on their rice and potato fields. Maintaining their own health and well-being and dealing with those risks.

The young mother could not communicate with me about her daughter's predicament, but one look and I knew this was a dire circumstance.

The toddler was burned on her face and arm from a boiling pot of water. The wounds were fresh that morning. For some reason, I happened to have a tube of suave and a tube of triple antibiotic and some pain relief drugs.

The treatment was palliative but I believe we helped. When we reached the first point of bus service to

Kathmandu, it was early and we were tired from long

hikes. We stretched out on the empty top of the bus and slept on our large backpacks. The hot sun finally made sleeping unattainable and as I woke, I was shocked with all the colorful people sitting around us. They had their knees in their chest and were cramped all around, not saying a word. There was a small goat, a cage of chickens, and bags of rice all tucked in about us. I quickly woke up Dave and we placed ourselves in among the crowd apologetically.

The bus was really speeding along. The brakes would squeal before the downhill curves, tilt, and lean side to side with the top-heavy load, accelerating again downhill to the next curve. Fear and anxiety could not be suppressed. When a small fellow climbed out the window and pulled himself up onto the roof, Dave let him have it, "You tell that son of a bitch to slow down or I'm going to kill him."

No one could understand but maybe the yelling did something to relieve Dave.

We rounded a curve and came upon a truck that had rolled over in the middle of the road. Of course, we walked around to the downhill side and boarded another fast bus on our way again. Racing across narrow bridges with pedestrians inches away. Grinding up wheat on the pavement that the farmers were turning into flour as the monkeys screamed from the trees.

Risk beyond our control but when it is done, 'a feeling of relief'.

*

In 1993, Terry was traversing a rocky cliff thousands of feet above the valley floor when she fell. We were on the slopes of a high and magnificent peak at some 20,000 feet called Ama

Dablam in Nepal. It is one of the most photogenic peaks in the world. We could see the expanse of the Himalayan Mountains and the far-off slopes of Everest from our position.

I was looking at another peak off in the distance, Baruntse, when it happened.

Terry's fall on the cliffs of Ama Dablam was caused by poor footing while stepping from one narrow ledge to the next on the side of a rocky cliff with crampons on. One had to wear these spiky boots because it would turn from rock to ice at any time. It seemed strange to walk across rocky slopes and climb rocky cliffs with these on, but when the terrain became ice, crampons were a lifesaver.

Crampons can get in the way though and create their own dangers.

John found this out when he was climbing a chunk of rock about 40 feet high along the side of the cliff. He was found struggling and tangled in the rope ladder, nearly upside down. Out of energy and just dangling there with his crampons all tangled up. After this incident, John gave up and headed down.

Problem was, he had the extra sleeping bag that my climbing partner needed that night at Camp II! We each had our share of loads to haul in order to build camps higher and higher on the mountain. It was the first but not the last time that I had to share a sleeping bag with another guy! All night, rolling and turning in unison to stave off the freezing night air. I had to do it again with Alan at Camp III. He had brought up his bivy bag, and that was it! He was running, laying down, inside his bevy bag most of the night, until I finally threw one side of my bag over him. We cuddled till morning, *ahhhhhh*.

Terry was clipped into a fixed rope when she took her digger down the cliff. She was in one spot and in a flash, a blink, she was in another spot, down the cliff. The rope is an essential part of being on the mountain. You have to rappel down in order to get down. Plus, the dangerous spots are fixed with a safety rope, secured at both ends. Unfortunately, we ran out of good rope and were left with using old ropes that had been left behind from other expeditions.

I was secured to such a rope while climbing from Camp II to III.

It was a steep, rocky scree slope. Loose rocks would tumble down with every step. I tried not to use the rope for pulling myself up, unsure of its strength. The ropes were lightweight poly. Like the kind you use for a tow rope for water skiing. They have a breaking strength of less than a thousand pounds and are easy to abrade on rocks. However, they are lightweight and come in long coils, hundreds of feet. Maybe good when they are new, but not when exposed to sunlight for very long, or left on a mountain for years. We should not have been using them, but we were out of ropes. I had to use this rope to rappel back down the slope the next day. It was faded in color, abrasions, and strands were popping out.

It was thin and just plain looked terrible! Three of us decided not to ascend the mountain again. Camp III would be my high point and it was a success all the way around. Camping in the snow near 21,000 ft. on the side of a cliff with magnificent curled snow cornices above me. It was good enough.

Terry was clipped into a good rope and of course it did its job. The valley floor was several thousand feet below her and thank God, she did not visit that spot. The anchors at both ends held like steel pins in rock should. She remembers thinking, *I made it to 20,000 feet and I'm not going to live long enough to tell my friends.* However, she was not done with her fun yet.

Further up the mountain, another ledge about two feet wide had to be traversed. Terry and Diane were climbing around this cliff, also, thousands of feet above the next piece of real estate. Her webbing that held her to the fixed rope became tangled around her ice axe on the pack behind her. She could not reach behind her to untangle the mess. She was stuck on the narrow ledge. Meanwhile, Diane is behind her freaking out, exclaiming, "I do not want to do this, I want to live long enough to have kids."

It ended in comedy and not a tragedy.

Terry and I spent one night at 20,000 feet and that's the highest point on earth that we have both been together. On Ama Dablam, the most photogenic mountain in the world.

Highest point Terry and I have both been together. Camp II, 20,000 ft. Cliffs all around 360 degrees.

Terry, before she fell.

Base camp. My dental office was in a back tent. Open for extractions. Camp III was in the snow, on a cliff, seen just above the clouds. (Dale)

Crampons and ladders don't mix well. On route to Camp II.

VIII

Cerebral edema is a life-threatening condition and many climbers have died at altitude from its grip. Many rescues and stories have filled the literature about these high-altitude adventures and life saving measures. Now I was part of the story at 24,000 feet on Everest. Later in 2014, I wrote,

Eyes

"I start the day with two lights, with one eye open or the other throughout the day one light dims; grey and grey as a cloudy storm approaches.

I see your figure and the color but, you are fading into a cloud or slipping below the water...The storm grows and the sea grows stronger the light fades, dims...slowly.

and the storm stays
but it only takes a day.
and the storm stays and stays.

Little is the light and the darkness comes
and you are gone,
gone for the rest of my life
with that one last light.

You were once a beautiful line of curves and depth,
your breasts had a soft contour of intrigue,
and hair giving way to the wind;

the depth has gone.
All the light has gone
what was once a bright blue sky and green grass is now...
only black;
losing one eye forever and ever...I have."

I often wonder if losing my left eye was a result of the pressure around my brain when I had so much edema at Camp III. Cerebral edema (I.C.P.) also restricts blood supply to the brain and thus, less oxygen resulting in headache, nausea, vomiting, dizziness, difficulty speaking, vision loss, loss of consciousness. I was dealing with all these symptoms and Scott had to deal with me.

Scott had done this show before though. On K-2 with Ed Viesturs, they were called on to rescue a female climber that had just reached the summit.

Leaving in a storm, they got flushed down the slope in an avalanche. Ed was finally able to stop himself and Scott from certain death. They would not have been out on such a day but rescue is just what you do.

After this rescue, another two climbers were also suffering from altitude sickness at Camp II; Rob Hall and Gary Ball. Rob was the team leader that was also on Everest with us now. They were brought off the slopes of K-2 which Scott called 'The Hall and Ball Show' but Gary died the next year from another pulmonary edema situation on another peak. Rob Hall died on this Everest expedition in 1996.

Pakistan

"K-2 is the worst mountain ever to climb!" exclaimed many mountaineers. 1995, we were on our way to base camp near K-2 to climb Broad Peak in Pakistan. Broad Peak is an 8,000-meter peak or one of the 14 highest mountains in the world. It sits next door to K-2, the second highest peak in the world. We toured the embassy in Islamabad, which was nearly overrun with violent protestors just a few years before. Osama Bin Laden was killed 120 miles from there in 2011. The place is filled with the Taliban seeking a hiding place from U. S. forces to this day.

I thought little of those political things as I peered out the window of the brightly decorated painted reddish bus. I was amazed and gawking at how tall and plentiful the marijuana plants were along the roadside.

We had to take the long, narrow cliff side highway up the Karakoram Highway.

It was a road mostly dirt and rough with landslides closing it for days. Now it is considered the eighth wonder of the world. It follows the mighty Indus River from which I could not tear my gaze. So big, powerful, and so steep for much of the way.

Views of the highest mountains in the world fill my vision and leave me in a state of amazement. The great mountain ranges all collide here. The Hindukush, the Himalaya, and the Karakorum. The ninth highest peak in the world, Nanga Parbat, can be seen from the highway.

We stayed at a teahouse where the cockroaches were four inches long. Tough night. We leave the highway and the bus for a two-day, dusty, rugged jeep safari to the last village called Askole. Here, I see one of Greg Mortenson's first schools he built throughout Pakistan. A small rock building about the size of a large living room. I encourage you to read his book, *Three Cups of Tea.*

I met Greg years before in Kathmandu, Nepal, and knew of his reputation as a climber back then. His reputation as a school builder for these remote villages was making world news until Jon Krakauer wrote his book, *Three Cups of Deceit.* Jon wrote this book after his book *Into Thin Air;* the book about our Everest expedition.

Jon claims that Greg had lost his way with his charity donations and much of the money was spent on Greg himself. Jon had given Greg $75,000 at one point, before he investigated Greg. Anyway, the school I saw in 1995 was full of straw and seemed to be used for animals. Even the locals boasted of having a new school.

Jon had called me and asked me about my meeting with Greg and the school I saw in Askole when he was investigating Greg. 60 minutes did a big story about Greg and it did not end well for him. I always thought he had a great idea though. Just lost his way!

*

On our way up the valley, we cross fast flowing streams and dodge rock fall on steep slopes where the path must cut through. The rocks I saw falling were as big as cars. Major rivers are crossed by the use of a Jola. It is a box you sit in attached to a cable, ten feet above the rip-roaring river.

Someone must pull a rope to get you across. It was a toll Jola. Ten cents.

The long trek up the Baltoro Glacier is mind-blowing. It is one of the longest glaciers outside of polar regions. On either side of the flowing frozen mass, the vertical slopes of the big mountains are enthralling as they immediately gain a ridiculous amount of altitude. About two miles of altitude! Elegant emerald grassy knolls flow along the glaciers' edge but abruptly give way to the rocky cliffs. If the cliffs are not vertical, then they are slopes with hanging glaciers or snowfields. Captivating and a jaw dropping, eye popper! I just love looking at big mountains up close; fetchingly handsome. Galen Rowell described it best, when he wrote, *In the Throne Room of the Mountain Gods.* I feel so blessed to have stood among these magnificent peaks.

This was another large expedition and the climbers and porters wound their way like a serpent to Concordia, the confluence of two more glaciers. A celebration of where we were and what we had to do took place by drinking congealed goat's blood. Tasty! The best way to get food up this high is to have the animals walk themselves to the dinner table. A small herd accompanied us on the trip.

Nine people died that season in the Karakoram. Six in one very bad day on K-2. Alan came over from his K-2 base camp and visited with us before the storm. He was the guy I had to cuddle with on Ama Dablam. Peter Hillary was also at base camp, the son of Sir Edmond Hillary, who first climbed Everest. I had met Edmond Hillary in Nepal when he was checking out his school in *Namche Bazar* and begged for his autograph (1993). I was impressed that his son, Peter, was there on K-2, the hardest and second most deadly mountain in the world, behind Annapurna. Out of 300 people that attempted K-2, by the year 2008, 80 people had died.

Alan and Peter did not attempt a summit bid in the changing weather. Scott said the bitter cold and the gale force winds contributed along with the high altitude to the six deaths. Alison Hargreaves, a famous climber from Britain, was reported to have been blown off of the mountain.

K-2

Our team had good success on Broad Peak and Scott had the climbers off the mountain before the storm hit. I had suffered some splitting headaches all night long at 24,000 feet and did not attempt the summit after that.

It was a long trek out and the jeep rides took forever due to the fact we had to build washed out roads. I finally arrived in Skardu in order to fly back, instead of taking the long highway back to Islamabad. It was a small airstrip. The ticket office was packed with Pakistani people in the typical white garbs with black vests and grey caps. Everyone had a black beard. There was no line and just chaos at the counter. It was like a big huddle five deep by twenty-feet long; a mass of people. I stood back as one single, lonely object in the center of the room. I fretted about even being able to communicate my way through all this turmoil.

How many days would this take? Would they even pay attention to me?

About ten minutes later, the attendant waved me forward and everyone turned and stared. The crowd got silent and parted to create an opening for me. He calmly worked through all the paperwork, gave me my ticket, and I was on my way. The room was dead silent. Whew!

IX

I was climbing with climbers on Everest who had reached the summit and survived K-2. Scott, Neal, and Anatoli were on our team. There was also Rob Hall and Ed Viesturs on other teams. I was, however, not in their league at all. Not even close. Like an altar boy to a priest, now and again, I got to ring the bells.

Camp III is on a snowy shoulder off of the steep icy slope on the Lhotse face. It was here later in the month, that a rock came zipping down from above and slammed into the head of a Sherpa. He survived and was rescued off the mountain. I would meet him in Namche Bazar as we shared the same helicopter ride out to Kathmandu. He lay bandaged and quiet on the floor.

When they finally woke me up at Camp III, I had been asleep for some 16 hours. I would have just remained sleeping, I'm sure. Scott and Neal had just arrived that morning from Camp II. I do remember Neal helping me get my harness buckled up right. I tried but it was all wrong. I was stumbling around quite a bit, but Scott was able to guide me to the rope we had to rappel down. He clipped me in and put me on a short lease to lower me down. It was cold but a nice day. The descent was time-consuming and awkward but he managed me well. We passed the frozen body below the icy slope and I stumbled along back to Camp II for several hours. I guess I could describe it as being very drunk and very weak but without having any booze.

Scott knew he had to get me lower in altitude as fast as

possible, so he had Anatoli and another climber, Lena help me the rest of the way. Above the Khumbu ice falls, I clumsily slipped down a slope and slid onto a snow bridge over a crevasse. My legs broke through the snow and I was held out of the abyss by the rope that Anotoli was holding tight. I do not remember much more about how I got through the rest of the descent. I think I crawled back over the ladders. I could have been the first fatality on Everest that year but I credit Scott for saving my life. He would, however, bring me down the mountain one more time a few days later.

That night, I rested and slept from the long journey down the slopes.

I saw bursting bright lights in my brain going off like fireworks on the fourth of July. I'm not sure I would call them hallucinations or just neurons firing off in my head. They were not violent flashes, more like a cosmic observation of the Milky Way on a clear night. Spooky!

*

So what else can old mountaineers do when they stay off the slopes but still search for adventure? Some might go down instead of going up, aka, canyoneering?

Sandstone patterns and textures that twist and turn in a narrow passage that you must walk through sideways like an ant in an underground tunnel, that is a slot canyon. The canyon walls tower above you for hundreds of feet and light can be precious but also makes the surroundings surreal, spooky.

There are illuminations of pockets, arches, and shadows in the overhangs. Light reflects off the pools and dances on the reddish rock wall beside it.

Terry and I walk along a narrow sandy path in Spooky Slot

Canyon. We must wade through pools of winter cold water and our down jackets scrape the sides of the canyon wall. It's an unearthly place to be in February, also very remote and without crowds. In fact, there are no people around anywhere, it's just too cold. Spooky Canyon is in Escalante Grand Staircase. What a great name, in a great place.

We duck under overhangs, crawl in sand, and squeeze through a few slots, like ants, except with a dog. After a while, we come to a wide spot and Terry is allowed to pass me. I wonder a bit about what I would do in a flash flood, where could I possibly go? But it's winter, so I reflect on other 'what ifs'. The 'what if' shows up right ahead of us.

The slot is only six inches wide at the bottom and about six feet up, it is one foot wide. It's like a funnel. We must climb up to the wider part of the narrow passage. Terry makes an attempt. Then I call her back. I fret with fear thinking of the potential problems and how remote we both are in this spooky place.

I related to her the story of Steve. He was a friend of ours from sailing days and had a bizarre life-threatening adventure. He must have had a similar situation as we were faced with now. He made a move and slipped down the funnel of the cliff sides and got stuck in the narrow slot below him. His feet were dangling above the floor and his body was stuck at the hips. It was too narrow to get any hand holds to pull himself up and no floor under his feet to help push up. There was no room to turn or twist sideways. His friend was unable to help. After many attempts and several hours, he was running out of energy and hope. He related to us about how low his spirits had become. He was accepting his death. After a dismal last try, he gave up for a while and started to think. Bam! Rocks, he needed more rocks. His partner began hauling in small rocks and dribbled them down the wall beside him. A long process, I'm sure. He was finally able to get enough under his feet to push up! Bit by bit, little by little, until he was free.

Terry and I left this spot for another day, a summer day. We did many other slot canyons in remote winter places. All wonderful, beautiful, bizarre places.

Terry, in a cold, isolated, spooky place in February.

Spooky, way below picture below.

Too cold, but no people.

More spooky places to explore, way below.

X

At Everest base camp, I recover for the next few days and I acclimatize better and get stronger. I sit in the warm sun with my book, chewing beef jerky and watching an occasional avalanche break off the slopes around me. I will make another attempt at the summit.

Scott is busy with preparations and meetings with the other expedition leaders. They decide that Rob Hall's team and ours will go together on summit day. Everyone is making their own preparations. Hall's camp doctor visits me one day and asks me to look at their head sherpa, Ang Dorje. He is having severe tooth pain. I have extracted teeth before on Ama Dablam and at Namche. I carry a syringe and Lidocaine and forceps. I should mention I was a dentist. In this case, I do not want to risk a post-op infection when he is responsible for so many people up on the summit push. I do some palliative treatment, medicate the bicuspid, and treat with antibiotics. He returns to his group of twenty or so Sherpa friends and they laugh, pat each other, and soak in the sunshine one last day, sitting below the prayer flags with the summit of Everest way above them. All things are calm before the storm.

I will relate to you the upcoming events from my perspective but if you want a more detailed account, it is worth reading Jon Kraukauer book *Into Thin Air* or Anatoli Boukreev's *The Climb,*

or Lena Gammelgard's *Climbing High,* or read accounts in Life magazine, Time, New Yorker, Outside, etc. Or watch all the movies *Into Thin Air, Everest,* IMAX story, which I think was the best.

There are more clips than you can see in a week.

There was and is a lot of controversy about the events, including the blame but I do not want to either create or be a part of all that fodder. Primordial soup gets really thick at this point, it's been simmering too long.

I was paid $20,000 to give my account to a screenwriter for the movie Into Thin Air and he asked me a question I will never forget. Aren't most climbers narcissistic? Well, yes. With all the back and forth, with all the blame passed around and self-importance, yes. That applies to me as well.

Though it's been nearly 25 years and I am just now getting around to my story.

After the film was made and before release, the producers flew me out to L.A. to participate in preemptive interviews. In a room filled with reporters, I sat with the actors that played the parts in the movie. The audience asked the typical questions; why, how, when, etc. It was a big deal to promote the movie. Other movies were being promoted all day long. Later that night, Terry and I had cocktails with many actors from the many films reviewed that day. Terry clung onto Drew Carey and all his jokes. I mostly was interviewed by more reporters.

The producers wanted me to return a few weeks later and do more interviews but I refused. Instead, they came out to me. In Denver, they had a live film room and I sat with Christopher McDonald, who played Jon Krakauer. News stations across the country would log in and interview us live on their program, or radio shows. We did this all morning answering all the same questions and over.

Since there were many different countries on Everest at the time, it was also worldwide news. In 1996, Everest was still a big deal.

Again, this is not a big Everest story, "This is my adventure story".

The film crews just became part of my adventure. Film crews from Denver and even New Zealand came to my home as well.

XII

It was time to leave Everest base camp for the summit bids. Everyone was again healthy and vibrant. I had doubts about myself, and though it did not seem quite right, I moved up. The walk to Camp I was not good; I was slow.

Normally, I was ahead of everyone and going fast. This time, I had a hard time keeping up or was passed. What the hell was going on? I felt okay but my body was not moving as it should. I decided to spend the night at Camp One while everyone else moved on to Camp Two. Tim and Charlotte stopped in and checked with me before moving on. They later told Scott at Camp II that I was not doing well. I was not doing well. I was wondering why I was so weak. To my surprise, Scott came all the way back down form Camp II to check on me and tell me I would not be going up anymore. He made a sagacious decision. I cried.

He insisted on taking me back to base. I said that I would be okay to go down on my own and not to stress himself. Anyway, I had made this trip many times before. He said, "Dale, you are one of my best friends and I'm taking you down."

We had another good bonding moment walking through the Khumbu ice monoliths. Even a better time at base camp when we reminisced, laughed together, and calculated the next few days. It was a good time. He was excited and confident about the summit attempt by his team. It was the last time I would see Scott.

Five days from that moment I would be running down the

Khumbu valley in anger and remorse.

*

Running down a canyon trail, along a river, or down a mountain is exhilarating. It's just something you do after that 'feeling of relief'.

You are pumped up and strong, indestructible. While coming off a climb in Nepal, a few of the climbers got into a competition with each other and the Sherpa. The Sherpa had big loads and we had heavy packs and the Sherpa would pass us going at a fast pace. We kept up, and it began to go faster and faster. Pounding our knees while jumping down the rocky steps and negotiating the narrow trail. The big packs bouncing on our backs. This went on all the way down the Amphu Lobsa Pass until we came to a creek, which allowed a nice cooling off and a drink. Then we moved on again, fast. At the bottom, we were surprised to have been beaten by Alan. He simply jumped off the pass, paraglide and all.

XI

After I knew Scott was in his final resting spot near the top of Everest, I ran. I ran alone and with my pack. I ran down the glacier, to Dingboche, to Pangboche, to Tengboche, and almost to Namche, I stopped. All day and into the night, I ran. I ran from demons and frustration. I ran with sorrow in my heart and deep distress in my mind. I ran with guilt. What took us five days to travel on our way up I ran in one day. I was mad, angry at myself.

Why did Scott have to walk me down the mountain when he needed to save the energy for his climb. Did I help drain his body down too much? Why wasn't I a better climber? Why did I need to be rescued? Why, why, why?

Death has an absurdity that can't be rectified in a story, it can't be explained.

In that last visit, Scott and I sought out each other with time to live. Really live. Sitting on a glacier below the highest mountain in the world. I slept with a profound feeling of relief that night. I did not see Scott the next morning when he bolted up to Camp II. In the next few days, the team had made Camp IV for the first time. I was monitoring the radio with anticipation and hope. They strapped on their oxygen tanks and left Camp IV around midnight. It was a long train of some thirty climbers from three expeditions. Right off the bat, there was a bottleneck at the balcony as the guides and Sherpa had not yet set the necessary ropes. Then another hour delay when they reached the Hillary Step. Still a bottleneck.

The turnaround time was supposed to be two o'clock but the climbers still kept slogging up. Many spent too much time at the summit. Scott was already moving very slow without using supplemental oxygen. He was on top at 3:30 p.m. and the weather was not looking benign, snow had started to fall.

I heard the radio broadcast and we celebrated their success. All seemed to be going well. Scott said, "God, I'm tired."

At this point, he was probably already suffering from pulmonary edema or cerebral edema or both.

My accounts from here are taken mostly from Jon's book *Into Thin Air.* Also from my discussions with my team after the event.

Lobsong Sherpa helped Scott down from the summit and they passed Rob Hall and Doug Hansen and Makulu Gau still on their way up. Lobsong could not get Scott to move below the balcony at 27,000 feet. After much pleading, begging, pulling, and attempts to revive Scott, he had to move on. Gau had collapsed here as well, after he caught up.

The storm was serious now and many of the two teams had got caught in the blizzard conditions, hundreds of feet from their tents, unable to find them. Some huddled together through the night at 26,000 feet. Some fell with exhaustion and died there. Jon described 'the storm abruptly metastasized into a full-blown hurricane and the visibility dropped to less than twenty feet.'

Ice pellets were slamming their faces, gloves were being blown off, and they had trouble seeing their own feet, much less each other.

Beck Weathers from Rob's team had collapsed in the snow, hand and face exposed.

Rob Hall and Doug Hansen were still above the Hillary step, 28,000 feet. Doug disappeared and was never found. In the next full day after the summit, Rob was able to talk on the radio and was patched into his wife in New Zealand. "Sleep well, my sweetheart," were his last words.

Andy Harris attempted to rescue Rob, but was never seen again.

During the night of the summit attempt, after the sky cleared a bit, Neal and Klev were able to find the tents and sent Anatoli to rescue the rest of the huddle. He failed to find them in the blinding snow on the first attempt. Not giving up and with no one else having the energy to help, he was finally able to bring in most of the climbers one by one. Beck and Yasuko were left as unrecoverable.

Everyone was exhausted, vomiting, crying, afraid, and had frostbite on their noses, hands, and feet. Daylight came, but visibility still remained poor. Hutchinson and a Sherpa were able to locate Beck and Yasuko.

He found them to be still alive. Covered with snow, hands exposed, their faces looked white, matted with ice. The Sherpa related that it would not be worth the risk for a major rescue and it would be unlikely they could reach base camp. The conversation continued back at the tent with the other climbers. It had to have been a heart-wrenching decision to leave someone still alive behind.

Beck lay there most of that day freezing to death, unconscious until he wasn't. He woke up! He got up. With his eye frozen, his arm frozen and his white porcelain face, he dragged himself to the tents! It took more than an hour to travel the short distance. Everyone must have been shocked; no one expected him to survive much longer. The storm came on again, even worse. Some tents were blowing off the mountain.

Jon wrote about what he saw the next morning, *"He was lying on his back across the floor of the collapsed shelter, shivering convulsively. His face was hideously swollen; blotches of deep black frostbite covered his nose and cheeks. The storm had blown back his sleeping bags from his body, leaving him exposed to the sub-zero wind, and with his frozen hands, he was powerless to pull the bags back over himself or zip the tent closed."*

"Jesus fucking Christ," he wailed when he saw me, his features twisted into a rictus of agony and desperation. "What's a guy have to do to get a little help around here?"

He had been screaming for help for two or three hours, but the storm had smothered his cries.

Beck was eventually rescued by David and Ed from the IMAX team and five others. Beck was able to walk under his own power, an incredible feat. A helicopter was able to reach him just above Camp I. It was the second time ever this had been attempted. Beck survived but lost his nose and many digits.

Anatoli also tried to rescue Scott and was unable to do so. I knew at base camp that it would be all over the news very soon. News organizations were covering the story from the start of the expedition.

I did not want Scott's wife to find out and worry in such a way. Scott had told me his best friend was Micheal Allison and when I talked to him, on the sat phone, he thought I was Scott and began to congratulate him for summiting. It was a difficult phone call.

While our team was descending from Camp III on the icy slope of Lhotse, a rock came hurling down and smashed into a Sherpa's head with the force of a hammer. Then another one. He went into distress and was unconscious for some time but was rescued by his friends.

By the time he was flown to Namche, I had done my run out of base camp and we both boarded the old well used Russian helicopter for the flight back to Kathmandu.

A few days later, I was at the airport that was jammed with reporters from around the world. Some of the other climbers were being flown out from base camp and were bombarded with questions. Since my face was not black from frostbite, I remained incognito.

Scott may have saved my life at Camp III when I was suffering from cerebral edema but he really saved my life at Camp II when he said he was taking me down for the last time. I can't imagine myself in the events that took place on the top of the world.

There are many more stories and so many rescues that are beyond the scope of the story, but I recommend that you read Jon's book.

When I arrived back home, I went to see the doctor about the tremors I was having. Not good to be a dentist and shaky. The neurologist spoke of a condition that is triggered by a terrifying event and mentioned a term I never heard before 'post-traumatic stress disorder'.

She medicated for the tremors. Over time, the mental and physical symptoms have subsided and I have given up drinking all together. I am still easily startled or frightened when someone approaches me from behind.

In my search for the reason why we seek such avoidable risk, existential risk, risk that is inherent in these events, I question it all.

The universe seeks positive entropy, disorder and the intellect succumbs to irrational actions. Our belief that we can control entropy.

Is it in the genes or is it in the environment we were raised in? Over-achievers? Or narcissistic, self-importance? Recognition?

Can we even place such logic into our decisions for such

risks? A narrative cannot begin to describe our actions.

Or is it a mere primeval antediluvian instinct? The primordial soup.

In memory of Scott Fisher, who was a part of so many of my adventures.

1996 Everest team.

The Longest Day

A few months after writing *Primordial Soup* I found myself in a mystical place surrounded by people with face masks and green gowns and very bright lights. They removed my shirt and started an IV. I could barely keep my head out of my chest and speaking took all of my energy.

It was the longest day of the year, summer solstice, the greenest day of the year and a perfect day to float the river. It also turned out to be the longest day of my life!

The river was emerald green and clear enough to see the rocks on the bottom rushing beneath the raft. Moe was catching brown and rainbow trout. Terry and Mimi were in awe of the landscape and shooting photographs at every turn, in another boat. Dave was rafting solo. Bald eagles flew by or dotted the trees with their white crowns.

I always thought of my good friend Ed when an eagle flew by. The day he died from complications of a previous stroke, I was driving down a country road and scared up a bald eagle from his perch. He flew right alongside my car window just twenty feet away and matched my speed.

For fifty yards or so I admired his beauty and power. I finally cried out, "Ed?"

Now on this long day of summer I reflected again about Ed, many times. I was, however, thinking of how it must feel to have a stroke. As I tried to step out of the raft my legs gave out from under me and I was having trouble speaking. It was tiring to speak. Dave and Moe helped me to the grass near the river and I lay there unable to move. My body felt heavy and thick. I tried to move my legs and they would barely respond. I was seeing myself from the outside looking back in and knew I was about to lose my mind. This mystical esoteric experience made me think of Ed and what he must have gone through and how I was heading down the same paradigm.

I thought of how I had to row into the wind and the heat of the day and I thought of the age of my body finally giving in to a cardiovascular collapse.

The drive to the ER was especially long and I forced myself to not lose consciousness. Terry kept asking how I was and I could hear her but it was hard to force out any response. Vomiting ensued several times alongside the road and I could hardly lift my head out the window.

I did feel this way once before some 48 years ago on the night before my wedding. Then, alcohol was easy to blame but now I do not drink.

I mustered enough energy to say, "I don't think I'm going to make it."

I truly believed I was going to die as I lost my reality and faded into a dark place with no noise. At the ER entrance two men lifted my limp body into a wheelchair and pushed me inside. It was just like in the movies with all the rush and helter skelter of questions and tests and curtains and big bright lights. I had my head in my chest, unable to lift it for very long.

Cat scan, I.V., ekg., blood pressure, respirations.

Terry was parking the car and more questions ensued. "Dale, can you lift your left leg?" I did.

"Can you lift your right leg?" I did. "Can you smile?" I did.

Then I began to cry because I knew only then that I was passing the tests for not having a stroke. I was happy inside. Then it also hit me that what I had done earlier that day had to be the cause. I had done it before and only had mild repercussions. I had to tell them immediately.

As they transferred me from a chair to the table I mustered more energy and forced myself not to go to that dark place again.

I said slowly and with only a mumble, "I...ate...a....pot......brownie."

Then my head fell again. The four docs and nurses stopped in their tracks and all seemed to say at one time, "Ooooohhhh, change of plans."

One of them asked, "Dale, do you do this often?" "No," I said as I dribbled out the side of my mouth.

With all the Covid-19 stuff going on I'm sure they were wondering if this was just another case of intensive care. When the truth came out they were just laughing inside.

Later, after I slept it off and started to feel better, I told them how embarrassed I was about the whole ordeal. I was in the ER from an overdose of drugs, unbelievable to me. But, not to them, they said it happens about once a week. Please beware of friends making homemade pot brownies. The dose can be highly variable!

I am so grateful to be able to float in the river again.

CPSIA information can be obtained
at www.ICGtesting.com
Printed in the USA
BVHW020753231221
624588BV00015B/236